LAST SUPPERS

LAST SUPPERS

*If the World Ended Tomorrow,
What Would Be Your Last Meal?*

JAMES L. DICKERSON

LEBHAR-FRIEDMAN BOOKS
NEW YORK

To my sister, Susan

Lebhar-Friedman Books
425 Park Avenue
New York, NY 10022

Published by Lebhar-Friedman Books
Lebhar-Friedman Books is a company of Lebhar-Friedman, Inc.

Printed in the United States of America

10   9   8   7   6   5   4   3   2   1

Library of Congress Cataloging-in-Publication Data

Dickerson, James L., 1945–
    Last suppers: if the world ended tomorrow, what would be your last meal? / James L. Dickerson.
        p.   cm.
    Includes index.
        1. Suppers. 2. Celebrities—United States. I. Title.
TX738.D53 1999   98-55744 CIP
641.5'3—dc21
ISBN 0-86730-758-7 (cloth)

Stephan Pyles' recipe has been excerpted from *The New Texas Cuisine* by Stephan Pyles. Copyright © 1993 by Stephan Pyles. Used by permission of Doubleday, a division of Random House, Inc.

Dr. Robert C. Atkins' recipe has been excerpted from *Dr. Atkins' Quick and Easy New Diet Cookbook* by Robert C. Atkins, M.D., and Veronica C. Atkins. Copyright © 1997. Used by permission of Simon & Schuster.

Book design by Kevin Hanek
Layout and production by Communication Graf-fix

Visit our Web site at www.lf.books.com

TABLE OF CONTENTS

INTRODUCTION

"If you were told that life as you know it was coming to an end tomorrow, what would be your choice of a last supper—and with whom would you want to share it?"

With that tantalizing question work on this book began.

"Last suppers" has a different meaning to different people. For Christians it is the supper of Jesus and His disciples on the eve of His crucifixion, and it is the cornerstone of their faith. For Jews it conjures visions of Passover and the ancient exodus from Egypt. (Old Testament or New Testament, food is always an integral ingredient in the ceremonial observance of transitional human experience.) For lovers of fine art it is Leonardo da Vinci's portrayal of Christ's Last Supper. For those on the opposite end of the human spectrum, those convicted of life's most heinous crimes, it is the last sustenance they will receive before being led to the electric chair, gas chamber, or gallows: "Give 'em a good meal and send 'em on their way."

For the celebrities contacted for this book, it meant giving just enough thought to a rather serious question to arrive at a tasty—and at times revealing—answer. Before beginning work on the book, the first question I had to ask myself was what group of people I wanted to target for my queries. Any group would have worked. I could have targeted funeral directors, for obvious reasons; dentists, according to statistics the most suicidal profession in America; cartoonists, the group most obsessed with death, at least according to my personal experience; or chefs, while they may know the least about death, they certainly know the most about food. Of that group, only chefs made the A-list.

For the remainder of my list I looked at a cross section of celebrities from politics, sports, music, television, films, business, arts and letters, and entertainment. I made phone calls, wrote letters, and zipped off faxes at a dizzying rate. Some of the celebrities I had met or interviewed previously over two decades of writing about politics and entertainment—yes, the two fields are more closely related than you think. Others I chose because of their notoriety or media visibility. Some made the cut for the most subjective of reasons: because I like or admire their work.

Once I had a few recipes and menu items in hand, I engaged in some shameless name dropping to entice other would-be contributors between the covers of the book. To my surprise, I received responses from celebrities who declined to be in the book because Bill Clinton was in it. From Hank Williams Jr. I received a handwritten fax that said: "Sorry Buddy, anything with Bill Clinton in it, I will not do!" From Leon Redbone I received a fax from the singer's assistant (actually she had written a note on my fax and sent it back) declining the request but wishing me good luck with the project. Next to Bill Clinton's name was a note in a different handwriting, presumably Leon's, that said, "Guy knows an enchilada when he sees one!"

Compiling this book has been more fun than others I have worked on simply because I never knew what to expect. Most of my responses came by mail, but many arrived via fax in the middle of the night and others by telephone at unexpected times. Cammi Granato, captain of the gold medal United States women's hockey team, called me from an airport on her way to Finland. She just wanted to let me know she had received my letter and would get a recipe off to me "ASAP." That's hockey lingo for, "I'll slap that baby in the net when you least expect it."

Karen McDougal, Playboy's 1998 Playmate of the Year, telephoned me from the Playboy Mansion in Los Angeles. I envisioned her in Hef's spacious pool surrounded by a bevy of Playmates in various stages of undress, all of whom were fighting to wrench the telephone from her, all saying they wanted to speak to James ... but saying it the way the women say it in the James Bond movies ... James ... James Bond. I never asked Karen what she was wearing. I naturally assumed she was wearing nothing.

I got a few surprises along the way.

One of my favorite "new" celebrities is Sarah Michelle Gellar, star of *Buffy the Vampire Slayer*. I'm not sure if I like her because she is a nubile blonde of uncommon beauty who could hold her own in a catfight or because she is a vampire slayer, a profession I myself have engaged in at various times in my career. Whatever the allure, I was disappointed not to receive a recipe from her, but delighted to receive an autographed photograph that read "Best of everything" and was signed "hugs and kisses, Sarah Michelle Gellar." Convinced that she wrote that message to me personally (wouldn't you be?), I booked a seat on the next flight to Los Angeles so that I could surprise her with hugs and kisses. Unfortunately, something came up at the last minute, and I had to cancel the flight. I guess it just wasn't meant to be. Sorry, Sarah Michelle.

A letter to the New York Yankees requesting a recipe from a player who had received a lot of negative publicity in recent years didn't net a recipe, but it generated a letter from manager Joe Torre offering the author a "free" official Yankees duffel bag if he sent him $27.97 for a one-year subscription to *Yankees* magazine. Sorry, Joe, but of all the things most needed by the Yankees, money surely is not at the top of the list.

From Helen Gurley Brown, the longtime editor of *Cosmopolitan*, I received a polite rejection, with the following explanation: "I'm not a cook and never have had company for dinner . . . if we do entertain, it's catered and I barely know what food is being served. It's going to be a wonderful book but I'm not the right person to be a participant because I'm just not good at food (except for eating and enjoying)."

Microsoft CEO Bill Gates asked his corporate communications director to send me an e-mail explaining that he was simply too busy with other projects to be thinking about last suppers (by that I think he meant his celebrated federal court trial), and Wendy's founder Dave Thomas sent word that he was busy working on a book of his own and had no ideas to spare. *Friends* costar David Schwimmer didn't send a recipe or menu, but he did send an autographed photograph (some friend he turned out to be), as did Indianapolis Colts quarterback Peyton Manning (I like his dad better anyway) and Heather Locklear (who sent her photograph directly to my publisher). Bluesman Robert Cray couldn't send a recipe because he was out on his Sweet Potato Pie Tour (at least his tour had a food theme).

After several attempts I finally connected with best-selling author Ann Coulter. If her name does not immediately ring a bell, her face will, for she has been a favorite talk show guest, who has been called the political right's answer to Jane Fonda. You can imagine my delight when I finally received a response from her. It was a hand-written note, hastily scrawled, that offered a recipe for her favorite alcoholic beverage. I won't spoil the surprise of her beverage (and why she offered it), but I will say that one of the ingredients was for something called "triple sex." Or so I thought. After savoring that thought for a while, I double-checked that ingredient with a bartender, just to make certain there were no ingredients that could be mistaken for "triple sex." Oops! As it turns out, Ann Coulter wants Triple Sec and not triple sex for her last supper.

Even my publisher's boss got into the act. Jim Doherty, former publisher of *Nation's Restaurant News* and co-owner (with Los Angeles mayor Richard Reardon) of the Original Pantry restaurant, sent me in an elaborate dinner menu complete with eight courses, matching wines, a 50-year-old Père Magliore Calvados, and a pack of Marlboro reds. "What the hell," he wrote. "It's my last supper."

Men, by a margin of two to one, out-reciped women. Psychologists and sociologists could have a field day with this bit of information. The inescapable conclusion is that successful male celebrities enjoy cooking and eating—and successful women do not. Do women feel that way because they think it is demeaning to be recognized for cooking skills? Or is it because, in their quest for success and recognition, they simply never spent enough time with Mom or Dad to learn how to cook? If you ever find yourself in the company of a very successful woman you want to impress, the last thing you should do is ask her what she likes to cook. To be safe, try one of the celebrity recipes in this book and dazzle her with your culinary skills.

What you won't find in the book are full-page layouts on some of the last suppers enjoyed by the bad guys of history. For those interested in a Rogues' Gallery of last suppers, I'll share that research with you in this space, so as not to taint the celebration and good humor of the celebrity contributions.

Adolf Hitler's last meal consisted of spaghetti with a light sauce, which he ate in the company of his cooks; by that point in his life, no one else would dine with him.

Ted Bundy, the serial killer who was put to death in a Florida electric chair, ordered a last meal of steak, eggs, hash-brown potatoes, and coffee. They say he did not clean his plate.

Before being hanged in a warehouse in the Kansas State Penitentiary in Lansing, Kansas, Richard Hickock and Perry Smith, the killers immortalized in Truman Capote's *In Cold Blood*, ate identical last suppers: shrimp, french fries, garlic bread, ice cream, and strawberries with whipped cream. Apparently, Smith did not enjoy his meal quite as much as Hickock and only nibbled on his shrimp. In the "strange but true" category, my research revealed that most convicted killers order shrimp before the life is zapped out of them. That strikes me as strange, but who am I to say what would make a proper dinner for a convicted killer?

Carmine "the Cigar" Galante, a well-read member of New York's old-school Mafia, was shot to death on July 12, 1979, in Joe & Mary's Brooklyn restaurant while he was enjoying a delicious plate of pasta. When the police arrived, Galante was covered with pasta and sauce but still clenching his cigar between his teeth.

What surprised me most about the last suppers eaten by deceased celebrities is that they were usually hastily prepared meals taken on the run. Princess Diana's last supper is one of the few exceptions. She is the only celebrity I came across who had a truly sumptuous meal before meeting her maker. Unfortunately, most of us will never really have a last meal. Most of us will be fed by sterile tubes and painful injections for days or weeks prior to our demise. That may be one reason why this book struck a chord with so many of the celebrities who sent in contributions. The Amazing Kreskin attached a note to his "last supper," stating that he thought the concept was "diabolically brilliant." Coming from a mentalist, that's high praise. Others voiced similar sentiments, for which I am most grateful.

The recipes and menu items in this book are tantalizing because, deep down inside, most of us realize that we never will have an actual last supper. Most of us live for food, but in the end it is the last thing on earth we crave. People facing their imminent demise usually request pain-killing drugs, loved ones, or one last view of a sunset. There is no record of anyone ever asking for a peanut-butter sandwich or a bag of chips or a plate of barbecue ribs. For most people, perhaps it is fantasy, not food, that is the true staff of life.

Please enjoy these recipes and menu items with my compliments, for you never know when or where your own last meal will take place. Nor will you know if someone such as me will take note of the time when you enjoyed it.

Let us dine and never fret.

—William Shakespeare,
The Comedy of Errors

FILM AND TELEVISION

SHOW BUSINESS celebrities aren't like you and me. For all their gregariousness with the media and their professed devotion to their fans—under controlled conditions—they are usually very private individuals whose lives are built upon fragile foundations of exclusivity and insulation. They have people on the payroll who are expected to stand between them and the rest of the world. That well-worn phrase "my people will talk to your people" is no joke: It is the reality of celebrity communication.

Even so, it has been the author's experience that most celebrities, once you actually sit them down for a heart-to-heart talk, are cooperative and genuinely nice people. Crystal Bernard, for example, agreed to send in her favorite pasta recipe during a telephone conversation, long before I even knew the title of the book. One evening my telephone rang, and it was Fred de Cordova, the longtime producer of *The Tonight Show Starring Johnny Carson*. I recognized his voice before he could identify himself, for I had grown up watching *The Tonight Show*, and Fred de Cordova's voice was imprinted indelibly on my consciousness.

De Cordova, or Freddie as he calls himself, called to let me know he had drawn up a seating chart for his last supper and wanted to be sure I didn't mind. Mind? It made my day. Can you imagine getting a call like that out of the blue? The phone rings, and it's Fred de Cordova. Or Rhonda Shear calling from her mother's home in New Orleans. Rhonda and I expended three telephone calls discussing her pajama party in great detail, although some of that time, it must be said, was devoted to my efforts to solicit an invitation to her all-night party.

CRYSTAL BERNARD

Actress

Whan Crystal Bernard left Texas at the age of 17 to go to Hollywood to pursue a career in show business, she was offered living accommodations in a toolshed out behind a Hollywood mansion. It wasn't ideal, but it was better than living on the streets. Two months later she landed a role in the feature film *Young Doctors in Love*. Bernard quickly parlayed that movie part into a series of television roles, including stints on *Happy Days* and *It's a Living*. Her most recent role was as Helen Chappel, the spunky, star-crossed lunch-counter operator on the long-running NBC television hit *Wings*. You wouldn't know it to look at her petite frame, but the common ingredient in her career has been food. She thinks food, acts food … and talks food. Once, when asked by a nosy reporter why she lived alone, America's favorite television lunch-counter waitress said: "It's not that I don't enjoy men or have never fallen in love. The thing is, why make a decision so early in your life when you're not fully cooked yet?"

Crystal's Pasta with Meat Sauce

2 tablespoons olive oil

¾ pound ground sirloin

½ pound sweet Italian sausage (squeeze meat out of skin)

½ onion, chopped

1 clove garlic, finely chopped

½ small can tomato paste

¼ teaspoon dried basil

Dash of nutmeg

Handful of parsley

1 large can crushed tomato

½ cup red wine

Salt and pepper, to taste

2 pounds pasta

Grated cheese

Heat oil in large frying pan over low heat. Add sirloin and sausage, and stir until it begins to brown. Add chopped onion and garlic and sauté. Add tomato paste and all herbs and spices. Turn flame to medium heat. Stir frequently for 15 minutes.

In a separate large pot add tomatoes and wine. Stir frequently over medium heat until it comes to a boil. Add meat mixture. Cover pot with the lid left ajar and simmer for 1 to 1½ hours. Season to taste.

Boil water for pasta with 1 teaspoon salt and a drop of olive oil. Add pasta and cook for approximately 5 minutes or until done. Drain all water from pasta. Put into server and add sauce and grated cheese.

DICK CLARK
Television and Radio Executive

To GENERATION X, Dick Clark is the even-voiced guy they see on television every now and then, hosting a variety of offbeat comedy shows. They even may recognize him as the guy who kicks off the New Year's countdown each year. It is doubtful they are able to associate him with the rocking music emanating from their CDs. Older Americans have a somewhat different perspective, for they know Dick Clark to be one of the most influential men in the evolution of rock 'n' roll. It was in 1957, three years after Elvis Presley made his first recordings, that Dick Clark's *American Bandstand* premiered on television and boldly transported rock 'n' roll into America's living rooms. The show featured interviews with recording artists, live performances—actually, the singers lip-synched to the records, but they were there in person and that is what mattered—and lots and lots of attractive teenagers dancing and clowning for the cameras. Watching television today, we sometimes find it difficult to believe that rock 'n' roll once was considered revolutionary, a tool of the devil himself, but in the 1950s and 1960s that was how most Americans perceived it. The individual most responsible for exposing rock 'n' roll to a mass audience—and making it what it is today—is Dick Clark. Many consider him one of the most successful television executives of all time.

Cajun Corn Chowder

Celery seed, to taste
Cayenne, to taste
Paprika, to taste
Coarse black pepper, to taste
White pepper, to taste
Marjoram, to taste
Beau Monde, to taste
½ cup fresh cilantro
2 cups chicken broth
3 cups nonfat milk
1 cup frozen corn
1 11-ounce can Green Giant Mexicorn
1 jar Progresso roasted peppers,
  drained and chopped
1 tablespoon olive oil
1 tablespoon butter
2 cloves garlic, crushed
1 cup chopped onions
1 cup chopped celery
Freshly chopped cilantro, for garnish

Mix celery seed, cayenne, paprika, coarse black pepper, white pepper, marjoram, Beau Monde, and cilantro together in small bowl and set aside. Mix chicken broth, milk, frozen corn, canned Mexicorn, and roasted peppers in a large saucepan. Add spices to mixture. (Important: the amounts of cayenne, black and white pepper, and paprika used will determine how spicy the soup becomes.)

Heat olive oil and butter in a frying pan and sauté crushed garlic, chopped onions, and celery. Add to liquid. Simmer 10 to 15 minutes. Let stand for 1 to 2 hours, if possible. Reheat and serve. Sprinkle a handful of cilantro on top.

FRED DE CORDOVA

Television and Motion Picture Director

A S THE LONGTIME PRODUCER of *The Tonight Show Starring Johnny Carson*, Fred de Cordova probably is best known to fans of the television show as the watchful guy in a suit standing over to one side with his arms folded. Carson played off his paternal presence and good-humored reaction to his quips and occasional barbs. Carson's on-camera exchanges with de Cordova made the producer's distinctive voice as much a trademark of the show as Ed McMahon's ever-present laugh. If his only claim to fame was as producer of *The Tonight Show*, which was on the air from October 1962 until Carson's retirement in May 1992, that would be enough to ensure him a place in television history. But de Cordova had a solid career as a movie director before ever joining forces with Carson. He worked with many of Hollywood's top stars of the past half-century, including Elvis Presley, whom he directed in MGM's *Frankie and Johnny*. Of his last supper guest list, de Cordova said: "If I lived after this breakfast … I would consider this the ultimate list of guests for a very special dinner."

Guest List

Me

Ava Gardner	Rita Hayworth
George Burns	Jimmy Stewart
Kitty Hart	Nancy Reagan
Milton Berle	Allan Carr
Lauren Bacall	Candice Bergen
Nick Dunne	Kirk Douglas
Joan Collins	Jennifer Jones
Jack Benny	Johnny Carson

My wife, Janet

Menu

Large glass of fresh orange juice

Kentucky ham

Two fried eggs

Rye toast

Hot Starbucks coffee

PHYLLIS DILLER
Actress / Comedian / Artist

Phyllis Diller was a late bloomer. By the time she discovered she had a gift for comedy, she was 37 and had given birth to five children and endured years of financial and marital difficulties. Encouraged by her husband, she shaped her miseries into a nightclub act, which she debuted at San Francisco's Purple Onion in 1955. Five years later she was performing at Carnegie Hall. Self-deprecation was the key to her humor. Nothing was considered sacred. In later years, when she decided to undergo plastic surgery, she incorporated those experiences into her nightclub act. Today her press kit includes a complete listing of the 17 plastic surgeries she has undergone. Says Diller: "I've had so much cosmetic surgery over the years that no two parts of my body are the same age." Incredibly, over the years she has been able to continue her stand-up routines while pursuing separate careers as a television and movie actress—*Splendor in the Grass, The Sunshine Boys, The Pruitts of Southampton,* and *The Beautiful Phyllis Diller Show*—a solo pianist with performances with more than 100 symphony orchestras in the United States and Canada, and author of four best-selling books. More recently, she has developed her talents as an artist, and her acrylics and watercolors have been well received by fine-art dealers across the country.

Guest List

Jimmy and Rosalynn Carter
George and Barbara Bush
Bob and Dolores Hope
Buddy and Beverly Rogers
(and my date) Hugh Hefner

Background Music

Bill Evans jazz CDs

Dress

Dressy comfortable

Menu

Tossed salad with vinaigrette
Succulent roast turkey
Country stuffing
Mashed potatoes and gravy
Candied yams
Cranberries
Pumpkin pie with whipped cream
Coffee
Candlelight and wine

EILEEN FULTON

Actress

IF YOU EVER HAVE played hooky from work, been laid up at home with the flu or a broken leg, or if you are among the millions of dedicated fans of daytime television, you know Eileen Fulton even if you do not know her name—for as Lisa in the long-running series *As the World Turns*, she is one of the superstars of daytime television. For 38 years, she has been making Lisa one of the most endearing bitches of the small screen. They just don't come any more manipulative, devious, or sweetly diabolical than Lisa. Says Fulton of her character: "I was out there lying, stealing, abusing people, and being a general out-and-out bitch back when Erica Kane [competitor Susan Lucci's character] was finger-painting in kindergarten." When not wearing her crown as "Queen of the Soaps," Fulton has forged a serious career as a comedian and dramatic actress, appearing in the film *Girl of the Night* and on Broadway with Hal Holbrook in *Abe Lincoln in Illinois*. She has written or cowritten two autobiographies and six murder mysteries, and recently finished her first romance novel, *Soap Opera*.

Guest List

My closest family
My maestro friends:
Tony Bennett, Bill and Hillary Clinton,
Charles Rangel, Ayn Rand, Picasso, Gandhi
(who would probably touch only the Evian),
Jacqueline Du Pre, Van Gogh (one would
have to keep an eye on all the knives on the
table), Gauguin (I'd like him to have bathed),
and, of course, a really good interpreter (so
that no bons mots would be lost to posterity).

Entertainment

A string quartet, playing Brahms,
Schubert, and Vivaldi

Menu

To be served at Lespinasse in the St. Regis
Hotel, New York, New York
Jack Daniels Manhattan cocktail
Lobster and truffle soup
(a Lespinasse signature, and at $35 a plate,
reputedly the costliest soup in America)
Salad of baby greens

At this point, guests take "a little rest"
for conversation

Guinea hen with truffles
(a second Lespinasse signature dish)
Chocolate soufflé
Courvoisier
Note: Each course would be served
with its own wine

AMAZING KRESKIN

"World's Foremost Mentalist"

For the past 30 years, the Amazing Kreskin has been dazzling audiences with sleight of hand, seances, and an assortment of mental games that often dance in and out of the murky embrace of parapsychology. He calls himself a "mentalist," and that is as good a description as any for what he does, for his performances depend more on his interactions with the mental perceptions of his audience than they do on any physical props or magical devices. He swears he cannot read minds, but his audiences usually leave with the impression that he can. During a recent appearance on *The Howard Stern Show*, Kreskin conducted a seance that left Stern proclaiming, "This is the most amazing thing I've ever seen." Johnny Carson was so taken with the performer that he scheduled him for 88 appearances on *The Tonight Show* and used him as a model for his own "Carnac the Magnificent" character. Despite a schedule that has him doing 360 live performances a year, often in casinos, where he has proved to be unusually lucky at cards, Kreskin continues to be a favorite television talk show guest who always can be counted on to baffle the audience with his mental sleights of hand.

Guest List

I would have Liberace playing the piano throughout the dinner, Bishop Fulton J. Sheen as the after-dinner speaker, Mark Twain and Oscar Wilde among the dinner guests, who, along with Howard Stern, would be the finest social critics one could find. If Liberace took a break, Al Jolson would come down the promenade and sing, to be followed by Bing Crosby. To round out the conversation at dinner, the greatest figure of the first half of the century—Winston Churchill—would join us along with the sharp, astute, and worldly presence of Dr. Margaret Mead. Incidentally, there would be no dessert. I would simply follow my meal with a second dish of spaghetti and meat sauce!

Menu

My two favorite meals are:
(1) spaghetti and meat sauce
(2) spaghetti and meat sauce

Being Polish and Italian, I have been known to possess a voracious appetite accompanied with a high metabolic rate that has allowed me to eat sometimes four or five meals a day without gaining poundage. If anyone dared to tempt me by placing on a buffet my favorite delicacies Alaskan King crab legs, a lobster tail, salmon, swordfish, roast duck, dark meat turkey, and spaghetti with meat sauce, I would gravitate to the latter probably not even touching the others.

KAREN McDOUGAL

Playboy's 1998 Playmate of the Year

KAREN McDOUGAL is a junk food junkie—and proud of it. "I eat out, and there is no gravy on my mashed potatoes," she lamented in the *Playboy* article that announced her selection as 1998 Playmate of the Year. "[In Hollywood] they eat their sushi and little vegetables. Give me red meat and junk food." The former kindergarten teacher says that when she left home, she got into the habit of calling her mother for her homegrown Michigan recipes for "real fattening stuff," such as pizza, lasagna, and spaghetti. As anyone can see in her *Playboy* pictorial and video, her mother's recipes have not altered negatively her 5-foot-8-inch figure or diminished her modeling career. Before joining the ranks of former Playmates of the Year Jenny McCarthy and Pamela Anderson Lee, the 27-year-old blue-eyed brunette got exposure as a Venus International Swimwear model. When the modeling career is over, she plans to open her own kindergarten. Odds are she won't have to worry about her students ever playing hooky at lunchtime.

I love food. It is my favorite thing in the world. Sugar-glazed ham is my favorite, but I have to make it or I won't eat it. The ham has to be cooked with crushed pineapple, cloves, and cinnamon on it. The candied sweet potatoes have to have brown sugar and melted butter and you have to mash them. I don't like chunks. Then you have to put colored marshmallows on top—pink, green, and yellow—and brown them a little. The green beans have to be cooked with bacon and onions and brown sugar. That's so good. That's the only way I will eat them. The green beans can be canned or fresh, but fresh is better. I have a no-bake pumpkin pie that I cook. It's creamy like pudding and it's really good.

Menu

Sugar-glazed ham
Candied sweet potatoes
Green beans
Mashed potatoes and gravy
Pumpkin pie
Pepsi

Guest List

My family... and Elvis!

Music

Prince

ROSIE O'DONNELL
Talk Show Host / Actress / Comedian

IN THE SPACE OF TWO YEARS, Rosie O'Donnell zoomed from a successful career as a stand-up comic and supporting role movie actress to international stardom as the host of the acclaimed *Rosie O'Donnell Show*. Success was sudden but not overnight. Following her 1984 television debut on *Star Search*, she spent more than a decade honing her craft in the trenches of America's comedy clubs. When *The Rosie O'Donnell Show* first went on the air in 1996, Rosie was optimistic about the show's potential for success but was warned that a talk show glut would make success elusive. Rosie persevered, committed to the belief that what she had learned out on the road as a stand-up comic—namely, the benefits of good humor and eye-to-eye contact with her guests—would set her show apart from those of her competitors. Time proved her correct. In 1997 she was awarded a Daytime Emmy for Outstanding Talk Show Host, an honor that was repeated the following year. As her competitors fell by the wayside, her show actually grew stronger in the ratings. Today, she can claim cosupremacy of the daytime airwaves with Oprah Winfrey. When Rosie was asked for a menu for her last supper, she responded with an envelope packed with four recipes, two of them prepared on her show by Vanessa Williams and Estelle Getty.

Spicy Bean Soup with Cheddar Cheese and Chili

2 tablespoons olive oil

1 small onion, cut up

1 tablespoon minced garlic

4 15-ounce cans bean soup

2 15-ounce cans cheddar cheese soup

½ cup bacon bits

1 cup homemade or prepared hot chili

1 cup water

Heat oil in a pot and sauté onion and garlic until soft, not brown. Add remaining ingredients. Let simmer for 35 minutes. Serve as a soup with crackers or serve on nachos with melted cheese on top or on french fries.

Veggie Burritos

(as prepared by Rosie O'Donnell and Peter Gallagher)

4 tablespoons olive oil

1 large Spanish onion, peeled and thinly sliced

1 green bell pepper, thinly sliced, seeds removed

1 red bell pepper, thinly sliced, seeds removed

2 cloves garlic, finely minced

1 28-ounce can whole, peeled plum tomatoes in puree, coarsely chopped

1 tablespoon ground cumin

1 teaspoon oregano

1 teaspoon basil leaves

½ teaspoon ground thyme

Salt, to taste

Ground cayenne, to taste

1 small zucchini, cut into cubes

1 small yellow squash, cut into cubes

½ small eggplant, cut into cubes, skin left on

1 14-ounce can black beans, drained and rinsed

1 14-ounce can chick peas, drained and rinsed

½ box frozen chopped mustard greens, defrosted

1 28-ounce can refried beans, drained and rinsed

6 to 8 flour tortillas, burrito style

1 package shredded cheddar cheese (optional)

1 package shredded Monterey Jack cheese (optional)

Heat 1 tablespoon of olive oil in a medium-sized, nonstick Teflon pan, and sauté onion, peppers, and garlic over medium heat until veggies are soft. Add canned tomatoes and include the puree with cumin, oregano, basil, thyme, salt, and cayenne to taste. Allow to simmer for 10 to 15 minutes over low heat. Adjust seasonings to your liking. In a separate pan, heat the remaining olive oil and sauté the zucchini, yellow squash, and eggplant until soft. Add to tomato, pepper, and onion mixture. Then add drained black beans, chick peas, and mustard greens.

Simmer for 5 minutes over low heat. Taste and adjust seasoning. Heat refried beans and put approximately 3 ounces of the refried beans in a soft flour tortilla. Then put approximately 3 ounces of the veggie mix in the flour tortilla. Sprinkle with shredded cheese and roll into a burrito. Brown burrito slightly under the broiler. Serve with rice and garnishes—guacamole, sour cream, and salsa. Makes about 6 to 8 servings.

Vanessa Williams Carrot Cake

2 cups sugar

1½ cups salad oil

4 eggs

3 cups grated carrots

2 cups flour, sifted

2 teaspoons baking soda

2 teaspoons baking powder

2 teaspoons cinnamon

1 teaspoon salt

1 cup raisins

½ cup chopped nuts

Mix sugar, oil, and eggs. Add carrots and mix well. Add flour, baking soda, baking powder, cinnamon, and salt sifted together. Mix. Fold raisins and nuts into batter and pour into two greased 9" round layer pans or one 13" x 9" pan. Bake in a preheated 350-degree oven for about 35 to 40 minutes.

ICING

1 8-ounce package cream cheese

¼ cup margarine, softened

1 pound confectioners' sugar

2 teaspoons vanilla extract

1 cup chopped nuts

Work cheese until soft. Add margarine and beat in sugar gradually. Add vanilla and nuts, and mix. Spread on the carrot cake. Enjoy!

Estelle Getty's "Hurry It Up" Lasanga

2 tablespoons olive oil

2 pounds ground beef

1 medium onion, chopped

2 tablespoons garlic powder

2 tablespoons oregano

1 tablespoon thyme

1 teaspoon pepper

1 teaspoon salt

1½ tablespoons seasoning salt

2 tablespoons dried basil

1 pound cooked rotelli pasta

1 13-ounce can mushrooms

1 28-ounce can chopped tomatoes

1 jar Prego sauce

16 ounces ricotta cheese

2 cups grated mozzarella cheese

Heat olive oil in a sauté pan and cook the ground beef and onion. Drain the fat. To the meat and onion mixture, add the garlic powder, oregano, thyme, pepper, salt, seasoning salt, and dried basil. Cook over low heat for a few minutes.

Meanwhile, cook the rotelli pasta in boiling, salted water. Drain.

In a mixing bowl combine the mushrooms, chopped tomatoes, Prego, meat mixture, and cooked pasta. Stir in ricotta cheese. Transfer to a casserole dish. Top with grated mozzarella cheese. Bake in a preheated 400-degree oven for about 30 minutes. Serve.

RHONDA SHEAR

Comedian / Actress

"THERE'S NO SUCH THING as a little body language when you're talking about [Rhonda] Shear, a petite, Barbie-shaped bundle of energy and intelligence which is likely to be overshadowed by other, uh, attributes," wrote the *New York Post* of the star of the long-running USA Network's Friday night series *USA: Up All Night*. In recent years Shear has had starring television roles on *Silk Stalkings*, *Happily Ever After*, and *Married . . . with Children*, and in the movies *Spaceballs* and *Basic Training*. Her start in show business began innocently enough when she appeared fully clothed in *Playboy's* pictorial "Girls of the New South." At the time she held the title of "Queen of the Floral Trail Society," one of more than 40 beauty pageant titles she captured in her home state of Louisiana, including Miss Louisiana U.S.A. When the Floral Trail Society rescinded her title because of her appearance in *Playboy*, she hired a lawyer and the resulting publicity was enough to catch the attention of Hollywood agents. Shear later appeared unclothed in a *Playboy* celebrity pictorial, but by then she had demonstrated undeniable comedic talents. Currently, she is touring nightclubs and casinos as a stand-up comic. She bills her act as Rhonda Shear's Pajama Party and features three other female comics. Her most recent entrepreneurial enterprise is a line of porcelain collectible dolls called the Shear Line.

I would have a very Rhondaesque last supper—an all-night pajama party. I would serve only junk food. I would have everything there a woman watches her weight for. I would want to have all my favorite women there (the same people a lot of guys would want): Marilyn Monroe, Madonna, Dolly Parton, Sophia Loren, Jayne Mansfield, Lucy, Mae West, Carmen Miranda, Joan Rivers, Phyllis Diller, Bridget Bardot, and Elizabeth Taylor. I'd also invite my favorite person in the universe, Barbara Eden, and, of course, my mother, Jennie. Elvis would crash the party in the middle of the night and perform with Ann-Margret. It would be fabulous. And there would be catfights during the night. My last supper would be a major diva bitch party.

Menu

Potato chips, guacamole, french fries,
onion rings, fried chicken, popcorn,
ice cream with tons of chopped nuts,
every kind of junk food you can think of,
lots of chocolate,
pizza with everything,
and maybe a big vat of gumbo just for me

BETTY WHITE

Actress

Betty White is one of the most identifiable supporting actresses of the 1970s and 1980s. The mischievous blank stare and singsong voice of her trademark characters are recognizable to anyone who has ever spent time in front of a television. Her Emmy-winning role as the ditzy, man-hungry, cooking-show host on CBS's *The Mary Tyler Moore Show* broke new ground in television's ongoing war of sexual innuendo and offered a perfect counterpoint to Mary's prim and proper character, who oozed with a squeaky-clean sexuality. White followed that with a costarring role on NBC's Emmy-winning *The Golden Girls*, a long-running sitcom that also starred Estelle Getty and Beatrice Arthur. Betty White belongs to a select group of actresses who have been able to sustain roles in separate television shows over a period of two decades or longer. *The Mary Tyler Moore Show* was consistently in the top 20 in ratings in the 1970s, and *The Golden Girls* held its own in the top 20 during much of the 1980s.

Chicken Wings Pacifica

1 stick butter or margarine

1 cup soy sauce

1 cup brown sugar

¾ cup water

½ teaspoon dry mustard

3 pounds chicken wings (or more—
   they disappear fast)

In a small pot, heat butter or margarine, soy sauce, sugar, water, and mustard until butter and sugar melt. Cool. Arrange wings in shallow baking pan. Pour mixture over wings and marinate at least two hours, turning once or twice. Bake in same pan in a 375-degree oven for 75 to 90 minutes, turning occasionally. Drain on paper towels.

VANNA WHITE
Television Personality

As cohost of television's wildly popular *Wheel of Fortune*, Vanna White has become a household name to more than 100 million weekly viewers, all without ever saying a word. Since joining *Wheel of Fortune* in 1982, she has remained an integral part of the show by doing little more than turning letters on the game board and applauding the efforts of the guests. Those who keep up with such things report she claps her hands an average of 140,400 times a season and has logged an impressive 332 miles by turning letters at the puzzle board. The key to her success is her charismatic presence, which she adorns in more than 200 different designer outfits each year. Before joining the show, she was one of Atlanta's top fashion models. When Vannamania was at its peak in the late 1980s, she published her best-selling autobiography, *Vanna Speaks*, which dispelled rumors that she did not possess an intelligible voice. *Wheel of Fortune* fans were concerned in 1997, when the show announced it was converting to a state-of-the-art electronic puzzle board. That meant Vanna was no longer needed to turn the letters. As it turned out, the fans' concern was unfounded. Today, Vanna points at the letters and watches them flash on electronically, and she's as popular as ever.

Cottage Cheese Salad

32 ounces plain cottage cheese

1 3-ounce box Jell-O
(I use lime flavored)

1 8-ounce can crushed pineapple, in its own juice

1 8-ounce container Cool Whip Whipped Topping, regular or lite

Put cottage cheese in a bowl, and then pour dry Jell-O mix right from the box over it. Mix well. Drain pineapple and add to mixture. Fold in Cool Whip. Refrigerate until ready to serve. You also can add chopped walnuts or pecans if desired.

MUSIC

MUSIC CELEBRITIES like to eat as much as the next person, but few learn to cook for themselves until they hit the twilight of their career. There's a good reason for that. In the years before they are "discovered," their lives usually are built around a schedule of one-nighters that don't leave much time for cooking. Once they make the big time, they learn the awful truth: Except for those few weeks each year when they are holed up in a studio recording an album, putting in 20-hour days, their livelihood is based on a series of one-nighters. If you are in the music business, it doesn't matter whether you are Alanis Morissette or the no-name wannabe at Bubba's Bar & Grill, your life is still built around one-nighters.

Despite the hardships of the road, musicians found time to respond to the last supper dinner bell. Gregg Allman's last supper arrived via fax (in the author's household, a telephone ring sends everyone scurrying to see what has arrived, sort of like children rushing to look under the tree at Christmas). Dr. John, Crystal Gayle, Billy Burnette, Paul Anka, Scotty Moore, Patti Page, Marcia Ball, Terri Clark, Rosemary Clooney, Helen Reddy, Brenda Lee, and Tom T. Hall combined their culinary voices for an all-star jam, the likes of which will probably never again grace the confines of a celebrity kitchen.

For road-weary recording artists and musicians who, over the years, have been exposed to lean times and all-too-frequent airplane crashes, every meal is potentially a last supper.

GREGG ALLMAN
Recording Artist

FOR YEARS GREGG ALLMAN has been heralded as the leading figure in the Southern rock movement. It is a label that baffles him and at times irritates him. "I don't know why they do that," says the Nashville-born rock legend. "It seems to me there are four kings of rock 'n' roll. One of them, Elvis Presley, is dead. The others are Jerry Lee Lewis, Chuck Berry, and Little Richard. Lewis is from Louisiana. Presley from Tupelo, Mississippi. Berry is from St. Louis, and Little Richard is from Georgia. Saying 'Southern rock' is like saying 'rock rock.' Rock 'n' roll was created in the South, just like the blues. It doesn't really offend me that much [that people would use the term 'Southern rock'] . . . but my brother used to ask, 'Why do they do that?'" Gregg's brother, of course, was Duane Allman, who was killed in a motorcycle accident nearly 30 years ago. Their double album, *Live at the Fillmore East* is considered by many music critics to be among the finest rock albums ever produced. After his brother's death, Gregg disbanded the group for several years to pursue a solo career; but he has since reformed the group and breathed new life into the Allman Brothers Band and continues to draw sellout crowds on the concert circuit.

Guest List

Ray Charles and his entire orchestra.

Menu

Catfish and hush puppies
Red beans and rice
Sweet iced tea
Tiramisu

PAUL ANKA

Recording Artist

P AUL ANKA was still a teenager when he had his first hit in 1957, a groovy teen ballad named "Diana." For the remainder of the decade, the Ottawa-born singer gave Elvis Presley and Ricky Nelson a real run for their money with a string of hits, including "Put Your Head on My Shoulder" and "Puppy Love." What made Anka different was the fact that he was a prolific songwriter, a talent that served him well in succeeding decades. Tom Jones had a big hit with "She's a Lady," and Frank Sinatra recorded what many consider his signature song with the Anka-penned "My Way." Incredibly, Anka has more than 900 songs to his credit, including the long-running theme for *The Tonight Show Starring Johnny Carson*. In 1998 he released his 123rd album, *A Body of Work*. The album features duets with some of the top names in popular music, including Celine Dion, Patti LaBelle, Peter Cetera, and Frank Sinatra, whose voice was taken—with his permission before his death—from a previous recording of "My Way" and blended with Anka's voice on a current arrangement. After 40 years in show business, Anka no longer gears his act toward the teen audience that made him famous, but he continues to be a major draw at casinos, where he commands multimillion-dollar contracts.

Warm Scallops and Avocado Salad

2 cups homemade chicken broth

¾ cup sea scallops

½ cup olive oil

1½ tablespoons sherry wine vinegar

1 teaspoon Dijon mustard

Salt and freshly ground pepper

2 platefuls fresh spinach, cut in a chiffonade or thin strips

1 avocado, sliced and sprinkled with lemon juice

Toasted walnuts

Heat broth to a high simmer—do not boil. Add scallops, cover, and cook until just barely done, about 2 or 3 minutes. Turn off heat and pour scallops and broth into a bowl that has been set into another bowl of ice all the way up the sides. Set aside until ready to assemble salad.

Meanwhile, in a small saucepan, combine olive oil, sherry wine vinegar, Dijon mustard, and season to taste. Heat to simmer.

Just before serving, remove scallops from broth and slice thinly into rounds. Make a bed of spinach on each of the 2 plates. Arrange avocados in a star pattern over spinach. Arrange scallops atop avocados, sprinkle with walnuts, and pour hot dressing over all. Serve at once. Yields 2 servings.

MARCIA BALL

Recording Artist

Considered by many to be the reigning Queen of Texas Blues, Marcia Ball ascended to that throne by a circuitous route that took her to Nashville in the early 1970s for a short-lived career as a country singer, then through brief stints with pop and rock 'n' roll, bumpy-road detours that eventually took her full circle back to the blues, the music that seemed to make the most sense to her. In 1980 she decided to devote her life to the blues. "More than any other musical style, the blues is a lifetime pursuit," she explains. "The older you get, the more revered you are—especially for a woman, the blues is a good thing to do." She finds that the blues attracts a more loyal female audience. Blues singers aren't threatening to other women, she says: "They're more like sisters than competitors." Ball's devotion to her craft clearly has paid off. She has garnered numerous awards for her albums, including the Beale Street Music Award for Outstanding Musical Contribution. In 1998 she released a critically acclaimed album with blues sisters Irma Thomas and Tracy Nelson; other albums include *Blue House* and *Circuit Queen*.

Guest List

A table for 12, please.
Shakespeare, Leonardo da Vinci,
Mark Twain, Dr. John,
Dorothy Parker, Bessie Smith,
Robin Williams, Professor Longhair,
Homer, Willie Dixon,
my husband, Gordon, and myself.

That was hard. I'd like to throw a
party for all the people I wish I could
talk to (actually, listen to).

Menu

APPETIZER
One cup of crawfish bisque like my Aunt Love in
Thibodaux, Louisiana, made

ENTRÉE
Shrimp from Mike Anderson's in Baton Rouge,
swimming in lemon butter and Worcestershire with onion
and lemon slices; good New Orleans French bread

SIDE DISHES
Sliced, homegrown Creole tomatoes with balsamic vinegar,
feta cheese, and fresh basil leaves; a pile of barely steamed
fresh spinach; horseradish mashed potatoes

DESSERT
My own chocolate bundt cake with pudding in the mix
drizzled with fudge frosting and surrounded by
strawberries

BEVERAGES
A glorious red Côte du Rhône; a cup of Cafe Bustello

BILLY BURNETTE
Recording Artist / Guitarist / Actor

B ILLY BURNETTE has rock 'n' roll in his blood. His father, Dorsey Burnette, and his uncle Johnny Burnette were musical contemporaries of Elvis Presley in Memphis, and went on to establish strong careers of their own, first as rockabilly artists and then as songwriters. Many of Rick Nelson's hits in the 1950s were penned by the Burnette brothers. With so much music in the household, it was not surprising that Billy would enter the music business at an early age. He was 18 when he released his first album, *Billy Burnette*. In the years since then, other albums have followed, allowing Billy to forge a solid career as a guitarist and recording artist. His big break came in the 1980s when he was asked to join the legendary band Fleetwood Mac. More recently, he has branched out into acting while continuing to pursue his recording career. He has done six movies to date, including *Saturday Night Special*, in which he played the starring role of a drifter. Currently, he is working on a rockabilly movie for which he wrote the film treatment.

Guest List

Marilyn Monroe, Jayne Mansfield,
Sophia Loren,
and a case of fine Italian wine.

Menu

Spicy Italian spaghetti

Spicy Italian Spaghetti

2 tablespoons olive oil
1 pound ground beef
½ pound Italian sausage, cut in rounds
1 large onion, chopped
6 cloves garlic, finely minced
1 16-ounce can tomato sauce
½ teaspoon Italian seasoning
½ teaspoon cayenne
2 tablespoons sugar
Salt and pepper, to taste
1 pound spaghetti
Freshly grated Parmesan cheese

Heat olive oil in a large pan and brown ground beef and sausage. Add onion and garlic and cook for a few minutes more. Add tomato sauce, Italian seasoning, cayenne, sugar, salt, and pepper. Simmer over medium heat for about 45 minutes or until done.

Meanwhile, cook spaghetti in boiling water. Drain. Top with sauce and Parmesan cheese.

TERRI CLARK
Recording Artist / Songwriter

CANADIAN-BORN TERRI CLARK was a major player in the music revolution of 1996 and 1997, which saw women recording artists outchart their male competitors for the first time in history. Her self-titled debut album sold more than a million copies, and her debut single, "Better Things To Do," went to number one on the country charts. *Billboard* magazine named her "Top New Female Vocalist" of 1995. Her second album, *Just the Same*, went gold in the United States and double platinum in Canada. Her most recent album, *How I Feel*, was released in 1998. With songs such as "Suddenly Single" and "Poor, Poor Pitiful Me," she has become a role model for women in the 1990s. For Clark, it is a mutual admiration society: "When I perform, I never put myself on [a] pedestal because I could just as easily be one of them watching the show. Just because I sing doesn't make me any more different. I don't feel any better, and I think they know that."

Yorkshire Pudding
(Clark family recipe)

½ to 1 teaspoon roast beef drippings

1 cup milk

3 tablespoons melted butter

3 eggs, lightly beaten

1 cup flour

½ teaspoon salt

Preheat oven to 425 degrees. Brush roast beef drippings into bottom of muffin cups. Place in preheated oven. Mix milk, butter, and eggs. Add flour and salt. Beat together. Remove muffin pan from oven. Pour mixture in hot muffin cups. Bake until golden and very puffy—15 to 20 minutes. The pudding will fall slightly while cooling. Excellent with roast pork or beef.

ROSEMARY CLOONEY
Recording Artist/Actress

OSCAR-WINNING MOVIE DIRECTOR Mike Nichols once commented that Rosemary Clooney "sings like Spencer Tracy acts," which is to say that she has a voice that is so powerful and natural that it is difficult to catch her in the act of singing. A successful big-band singer, she made the transition to television in the early-to-mid-1950s as a costar of the Emmy-winning *Your Hit Parade*, a popular musical variety show that offered the hits of the day performed by the show's cast members. Over the years she has continued to make records. In 1989 a critic reviewing her album *Show Tunes* for *Forbes* magazine described it as "brilliant" and said of her voice: It has that "appealing aged quality, a little dry, a little short of breath, but very wise and sympathetic." Today, Clooney, who often is called "the best of the old school" singers, still records and still takes an occasional acting role. Younger fans know her as the aunt of actor George Clooney, who affectionately calls her Aunt Rosie.

Chicken à la Rosie

1 whole chicken, cut up
1 tablespoon olive oil
1 onion, chopped
1 green pepper, chopped
2 cloves garlic, minced
½ pound mushrooms, sliced
2 cups ketchup
2 cups chicken broth
1 tablespoon Worcestershire sauce
1 teaspoon black pepper
Salt and pepper, to taste

Put chicken in baking dish and set aside. Heat olive oil in a frying pan, and sauté onion, green pepper, garlic, and mushrooms until they turn golden brown. Separately, combine the ketchup, chicken broth, Worcestershire sauce, and pepper. Mix together and pour over sautéed vegetables in a frying pan. Let the vegetables and the sauce come to a bubble; then pour over the chicken. Place chicken in a preheated 350-degree oven and bake for about 1 to 1½ hours.

A little red wine can be added, if desired, while baking. Serve over rice or noodles.

CRYSTAL GAYLE

Recording Artist

WITH HER DARK, knee-length hair and striking facial features, Crystal Gayle added a much-needed touch of glamour to country music during the 1970s. Her lyrical, middle-of-the-road music seemed equally incongruous with the hard-edged tearjerkers that dominated the charts of that era. There were those in Nashville who thought that she was flirting with disaster, but it was a formula that worked, and by the end of the decade she was an international star. With the release of her album *We Must Believe in Magic*, which spawned her number one hit "Don't It Make My Brown Eyes Blue," she broke new ground with the first album by a female country artist ever to sell more than a million copies. That feat resulted in Top Female Vocalist awards from the Grammys, the Academy of Country Music, and the Country Music Association. Before the decade was over, she would make history again by becoming the first female country artist to host her own television special. That she would become an innovator and a symbol for women's rights in the music industry may have surprised the country music establishment, but it hardly came as a shock to her family. Her sister is country music superstar Loretta Lynn.

Pasta with Shrimp

3 tablespoons olive oil

4 cloves garlic, chopped

1 pound fresh shrimp, peeled, cleaned, deveined

One box angel hair pasta, cooked

Salt to taste

Heat olive oil in a pan and sauté chopped garlic and shrimp until done. Pour over cooked pasta, toss well, and add salt to taste. Enjoy with a tossed salad.

TOM T. HALL

Recording Artist/Songwriter

Tom T. Hall has had his share of number one and Top 10 records on the country charts, but it probably will be his songs that earn him a prominent place in music history. Among his hits: "Harper Valley P.T.A.," recorded by Jeannie C. Riley; "The Year That Clayton Delaney Died"; and "Old Dogs, Children and Watermelon Wine." The common thread that runs through all of his songs is his devotion to a strong narrative technique. He likes his songs to tell a story. Few tunesmiths ever have been able to match his sparse, lyrical style, and that is probably because his devotion to the written word preceded his interest in music. As a student at Roanoke College in Virginia, he planned to pursue a career in journalism. He enjoyed music, but it never occurred to him that words set to music ever could compete in popularity with the works of favorite authors, such as Ernest Hemingway and Mark Twain. Only after his career as a journalist was sidetracked by a job with a local radio station did he start channeling his talents into music. With the success of "Harper Valley P.T.A." in 1968, Hall's career took off, and he never looked back.

Tom T. Hall's Skinny Chili

2 tablespoons oil
2 pounds ground beef
2 6-ounce cans tomatoes
1 6-ounce can tomato paste
1 6-ounce can pimentos
3 6-ounce cans red kidney beans
Chili powder, to taste
Salt and pepper, to taste
3 medium onions, chopped
3 stalks celery, chopped
3 green bell peppers, chopped

Heat oil in skillet and brown ground beef, stirring until crumbly; drain. Combine ground beef, tomatoes, tomato paste, pimentos, and beans in a stockpot, and mix well. Simmer for 2 to 3 hours. Add chili powder, salt, and pepper. Mix well. Add onions, celery, and green peppers. Cook for 20 minutes longer or just until vegetables are crisp-tender for a crunchy texture. Serve with corn bread or crackers. Yields 8 servings.

DR. JOHN
Recording Artist

For a time, Mac Rebennack performed under the name Dr. John the Night Tripper. Onstage, he wore spangled robes and an ornate feathered headdress and adorned himself with gaudy necklaces. He drew upon his New Orleans roots to create music he called voodoo rock. But that was back in the days of psychedelic rock, underground radio, and counterculture lifestyles. With time he dropped the Night Tripper moniker and stuck with the more mundane Dr. John, although he continued to merge his fascination with voodoo into his soulful music. Over the years the pianist has attracted a cult following for his special brand of Cajun-flavored rock 'n' roll. In 1994 he published an autobiography, *Under a Hoodoo Moon*. Today, approaching 60 years of age, he continues to perform, delighting audiences with his unique voice and nimble keyboard virtuosity. In a pinch he'll still answer to the name Night Tripper.

Guest List

Eve, Mary Magdalene, Virgin Mary,
Ava Gardner, Jean Harlow,
Marlene Deitrich, Mata Hari,
Ruth Dominguez, Lucille Bogen,
Memphis Minnie, Lydia Rebennack,
and Catherine the Great.

Menu

Broiled crawfish
Raw oysters
Panne veal over speckled trout filé with dirty rice
Collard greens
Candied yams
Blackberry cobbler à la mode with Creole cream
Cheese ice cream
Barq's root beer

BRENDA LEE
Recording Artist

WHEN 5-YEAR-OLD BRENDA LEE began her singing career in 1949 at a county fair in Conyers, Georgia, she was only doing what came naturally. From the time she could talk, she had a unique talent for being able to repeat a song, note for note, word for word, after hearing it only one time. By the age of 12, she had a recording contract with Decca Records and was well on her way to international stardom. In 1960 her first number one hit, "I'm Sorry," established her as the most dominant female recording artist on the charts. For the first half of that decade both *Billboard* and *Cashbox* named her the most programmed female vocalist on radio. By the time her second number one hit, "I Want to Be Wanted," was released, she was knocking the most dominant males of the era off the charts. Elvis Presley, Chubby Checker, and the Drifters all took a backseat to the child prodigy who was dubbed "Little Miss Dynamite." Today, Brenda Lee maintains a busy schedule, often averaging 200 performances a year.

Guest List

My husband, my two children
and their families, my close friends,
my mother, my siblings and their
families, my mother-in-law, and my
husband's siblings and
their families.

Menu

Caesar salad

Escargot in the shells

Veal piccata

Asparagus sauté

New potatoes with parsley
(or sour cream mashed potatoes)

Stuffed mushrooms

Hard French rolls

New York–style cheesecake

A good dry white wine

SCOTTY MOORE
Guitarist / Coinventor, Rock 'n' Roll

In the beginning the Blue Moon Boys were a trio—Elvis Presley, Bill Black, and Scotty Moore. When they went into Memphis Recording Service, the home of fledgling Sun Records, on the evening of July 4, 1954, they had nothing more earth shattering on their minds than conducting an audition strong enough to attract the attention of record label owner Sam Phillips. In their enthusiasm they invented rock 'n' roll. Elvis's soulful voice, Bill's steady bass rhythms, and Scotty's impeccable guitar licks, best exemplified by his "Mystery Train" theme song, changed American music in ways that are still being felt today. Rolling Stones guitarist Keith Richards once said that while everyone else of his generation wanted to be Elvis, he always wanted to be Scotty. The only surviving founder of rock 'n' roll—Bill died in 1965 and Elvis in 1977—Scotty continues to record and perform. "Goin' Back to Memphis," a song from his critically acclaimed album *All the King's Men*, was nominated for a Grammy in 1998, and his autobiography, *That's Alright, Elvis*, cowritten with the author of this book, was a finalist for the 1998 Ralph J. Gleason Award. Moore is the only person ever to be nominated for both a Grammy and a literary award in the same year. All these years later he's still making history.

Mystery Train Deluxe

Peanut butter, smooth or crunchy
Sandwich bread
Saltine crackers
Pickles, sweet or dill

Spread peanut butter on single slice of sandwich bread; then crumble crackers on top of the peanut butter. Arrange pickles on top of the cracker bed. Place second slice of bread on top and enjoy! Says Scotty about this recipe: "Someone once asked me, 'Why the crackers?'" Scotty chuckles at the question. "So it won't stick to your mouth!"

PATTI PAGE
Recording Artist

IF YOU'VE EVER HEARD "Tennessee Waltz" or "How Much is That Doggie in the Window," chances are that it was the version recorded by Patti Page, who made the songs two of the biggest hits of the 1950s. "Tennessee Waltz" eventually sold more than three million copies and would have qualified the singer for a multiplatinum record, except that the awards were not put into place until 1958. She was a frequent guest on *The Ed Sullivan Show* during its glory years, and for a time she hosted her own network television show. The emergence of rock 'n' roll curtailed her recording career somewhat, but throughout the 1960s and 1970s she continued to make the charts with new recordings, including her 1963 hit, "Say Wonderful Things." In the mid-1970s, she recorded a number of country albums, several of which made the charts. She maintained a busy touring schedule into the 1980s and today lives in California.

Rice Casserole

2 cups Uncle Ben's rice

4 cups cold consommé, or 4 bouillon cubes dissolved in 4 cups boiling water—cool before using

1 bunch green onions, chopped

1 stick (¼ pound) butter or margarine

1 tablespoon Accent

1 8-ounce can mushrooms, stems and pieces (include the liquid in the measured 4 cups of consommé)

1 cup grated cheese—Parmesan, American, whatever you like

Place the ingredients into a large casserole. Sprinkle grated cheese on top and bake for 1 hour and 10 minutes in a preheated 350-degree oven. Stir just before serving.

HELEN REDDY
Recording Artist/Actress

PROBABLY BEST KNOWN for her 1970s hits "I Am Woman," "Delta Dawn," and "Angie Baby," Helen Reddy has focused in recent years more on her acting career. She appeared on Broadway in the mid-1990s in the musical *Blood Brothers,* and she subsequently toured with Willy Russell's comedy *The Arizona Republic.* She never seemed to pursue openly a role as a spokeswoman for the feminist movement, but it came with the territory with the release of "I Am Woman." The song was a number one hit and earned Reddy a Grammy. Ironically, it was a song that no one wanted her to record. Her record label hated the song. Her producer thought it would result in Reddy's being called a lesbian. Her friends told her it would destroy her career. However, she refused to back away from the song. She wanted to be identified with songs that projected a positive image for women. When she accepted the Grammy for the song, she shocked some people with her comments. "I want to thank everyone concerned at Capitol Records; my husband and manager, Jeff Wald, because he makes my success possible," she said, adding, "And God because She makes everything possible."

Menu

Fresh raspberries with hot rum vanilla custard

POLITICS AND BUSINESS

THE FIRST *LAST SUPPERS* query went to President Bill Clinton, whom I had met back in the early to mid-1980s while working as a journalist at a Southern newspaper that covered Arkansas politics. Like most people who have ever met Bill Clinton, I liked him as a person. As an editorial writer I wrote opinion pieces that supported his policies. When I sent him a letter requesting a last supper, he was in the midst of the Kenneth Starr investigation, so I figured that if I received a recipe from the president, with all the distractions he was facing at the time, it would be a good omen for the project.

The second query went to Senate Majority Leader Trent Lott, Bill Clinton's archenemy—at least politically. That part was mere coincidence, and no effort was made to pair them off in the book. I knew Lott from the days when we both attended the University of Mississippi. Even then Lott was personable, political by nature, and inclined toward consensus building. Over the years, going all the way back to the early 1970s, I have had occasion to write the senator, urging him to support various political issues of one kind or another, most of which I knew the senator opposed. Always, though, he responded.

If you are wondering why the business executives included in this section are here—and why some others are not—it is because they were chosen on the basis of their media visibility and the familiarity of their businesses to a wide segment of American consumers. George Zimmer, the founder of The Men's Wearhouse, is on television more often than Bill Clinton and Trent Lott combined. Abe Gustin and Dan Evins may not be household names, but in some parts of the country, their restaurants seem to be located on every street corner and interstate exit ramp. They are celebrities by virtue of their business and entrepreneurial genius, which has affected the lives of millions.

BILL CLINTON

President of the United States

Pᴿᴱˢᴵᴰᴱᴺᵀ Bɪʟʟ Cʟɪɴᴛᴏɴ has received his share of playful criticism from political pundits and comedians who have noted his tendency to frequent fast-food franchises while out on his campaign trail. Late-night talk show hosts have built entire comedy routines around his reported appetite for hamburgers, pizzas, and french-fried potatoes. In truth, Clinton's eating habits probably closely reflect those of the overachieving baby boomer generation that put him in office. When the author sent a request to the White House in the summer of 1998 for a last supper recipe, he was not sure what to expect, given the political trauma the president was experiencing at the time. Ever the dedicated baby boomer, Clinton briefly put aside the pressures of his office and responded with a recipe that reflects the Tex Mex–Southern tradition of his home state's cuisine. The recipe arrived the week before the president ordered a missile attack against suspected terrorists in Afghanistan. The author would like to think that the president, while studying maps of the rugged Afghan terrain and still tirelessly fending off attacks on his character from unforgiving pre– and post–baby boomer diners, ventured into the White House kitchen late one night to whip up a batch of chicken enchiladas to ease the pain. If so, it's what battle-scarred baby boomers would call character.

Bill Clinton's Chicken Enchiladas

Cooking oil

2 4-ounce cans chopped green chilies

1 large clove garlic, minced

1 28-ounce can tomatoes

2 cups chopped onion

2 teaspoons salt

½ teaspoon oregano

3 cups shredded cooked chicken

2 cups dairy sour cream

2 cups grated cheddar cheese

15 corn or flour tortillas

Preheat oil in a skillet. Sauté chopped chilies with minced garlic in oil. Drain and break up tomatoes; reserve ½ cup fluid. To chilies and garlic, add tomatoes, onion, 1 teaspoon salt, oregano, and reserved tomato liquid. Simmer uncovered until thick, about 30 minutes. Remove from skillet and set aside.

Combine chicken with sour cream, grated cheese, and other teaspoon of salt. Heat ⅓ cup of oil; dip tortillas in oil until they become limp. Drain well on paper towels. Fill tortillas with chicken mixture; roll up and arrange side by side, seam down, in a 9" x 13" x 2" baking dish. Pour tomato mixture over enchiladas and return to oven at 250 degrees until heated thoroughly (about 20 minutes). Yields 15 enchiladas.

ANN COULTER
Political Commentator / Author / Attorney

ANN CoULTER has been labeled one of the "radical chicks" of the political right and that "willowy and acid-tongued blonde" who writes a column for the conservative weekly *Human Events*. But the opinion-ated lawyer, whose book *High Crimes and Misdemeanors* was a national best-seller in 1998, has countered that spurious labeling with frequent appearances on *Politically Incorrect* and on MSNBC. Despite the label as a leggy spokesperson for the right, her credentials are impressive. After serving as a law clerk for a federal judge in the Eighth Circuit Court of Appeals in the late 1980s and for a prestigious New York law firm in the early 1990s, she worked as counsel to the Senate Judiciary Committee where she handled crime issues and drafted bills, amend-ments, and floor statements. The fact that she is not totally without a sense of humor can be seen in her choice of attire at a charity "shoot off" at a Washington-area firing range—she wore skintight jodhpurs with an ammu-nition belt clinging to her hips—and her choice of a last supper, which she explained by saying, "I eat out a lot."

Margaritas

⅓ tequila
⅓ lime juice
⅓ Triple Sec
Sugar

Mix all the ingredients together, drink, and enjoy.

DAN W. EVINS

Chairman and CEO, Cracker Barrel

IN 1969 DAN EVINS got a dandy idea. His Shell Oil service station was doing pretty good business, but he wondered if maybe it might do even better if he opened up a restaurant at the same location. He named the restaurant the Cracker Barrel Old Country Store. The concept went over so well that he quickly opened up additional gas stations and restaurants. Who would have thought people would want to have dinner at the same place they filled up with gas? Evins did—and he was right. When the gas crunches of the 1970s started choking the life out of many service stations, Evins started dropping the gas pumps and focusing on his successful restaurants. Incredibly, sales increased without the gas pumps. The restaurants, which feature a rustic, country-store design and a gift section, offer made-from-scratch cooking and a Southern menu that includes barbecue ribs, biscuits, turnip greens, and grits. Today, the Tennessee-based company operates more than 260 roadside restaurants and gift shops, mostly in the eastern United States, with sales exceeding $1 billion a year.

Ragu Bolognese

4 tablespoons butter

¼ pound smoked ham, coarsely chopped (about 1 cup)

1 cup coarsely chopped onion

¼ cup coarsely chopped carrots

½ cup coarsely chopped celery

2 tablespoons olive oil

¾ pound twice-ground beef

¼ pound lean twice-ground pork

½ cup dry white wine

2 cups beef stock

2 tablespoons tomato paste

½ pound chicken livers

1 cup heavy cream

Pinch of nutmeg

Salt

Freshly ground black pepper

Cooked pasta

Melt 2 tablespoons butter in a heavy skillet over moderate heat. Add ham, onions, carrots, and celery and cook until browned, about 10 minutes. Transfer mixture to a 3- or 4-quart saucepan. Heat olive oil in skillet and brown the beef and pork over moderate heat, stirring constantly. Add wine and increase the heat. Stir until most of the liquid has boiled away. Add meat to the vegetable mixture and stir in the stock and tomato paste. Bring to a boil; then reduce heat and simmer for about 45 minutes. Over high heat melt remaining 2 tablespoons butter and add chicken livers. Cook for about 4 minutes or until browned. Chop the chicken livers into small pieces and save them until you are ready to add to the sauce—about 10 minutes before it is cooked. Just before serving, stir in the cream and heat. Season with nutmeg, salt, and pepper. Serve on pasta.

ABE GUSTIN JR.

Chairman, Applebee's Neighborhood Grill & Bar

ABE GUSTIN JR. is one of the principal shareholders and chairman of the board of Applebee's International, Inc., an Overland Park, Kansas–based casual-dining restaurant chain that has more than 750 Applebee's Neighborhood Grill & Bar locations. With annual sales estimated to exceed $1 billion—including franchises—in 45 states, Canada, the Netherlands, and the Caribbean, Applebee's is considered one of the most successful casual-dining restaurant chains in the United States. For the past several years, the company has opened more than 100 new restaurants a year, with franchises earmarked for Germany, Sweden, and Belgium. Before getting into the restaurant business in 1983, Gustin served as chairman, president, and director of ABA Distributors, a wholesale beer distributor located in Kansas City.

Guest List

Linda Gustin, my wife;
Mr. and Mrs. Abe Gustin,
my parents; Mr. and Mrs. Lloyd Hill,
CEO Applebee's International;
Mr. and Mrs. Bob Martin,
executive vice president, marketing,
Applebee's International;
Mr. and Mrs. Tom Roupas, retired
former boss and vice president,
Schlitz Brewing; his five brothers
and their spouses:
Blackie and Sue Durham,
Fred and Mary Jo Gustin, Ray and Jo
Gustin, Bebe and Paul Lindsey,
and Doug and Elizabeth Scherl;
Arnold Palmer; and Lee Iacocca.

Menu

Almond fried shrimp

Almond Fried Shrimp

PREPARATION OF SHRIMP

21 to 25 shrimp, peeled, deveined,
  butterflied, tail on
Seasoned flour
Egg wash
Almond-seasoned crumbs
3 cups light cooking oil
Orange amaretto sauce

Dredge shrimp in seasoned flour, shaking off excess. Holding shrimp by tail, dip into egg wash. Allow excess to drain, and then place shrimp in pan of almond-seasoned crumbs. Lightly roll shrimp in crumbs and shake off excess. Lay shrimp on parchment-lined sheet pan and set aside in refrigerator.

Meanwhile, heat cooking oil to about 250 degrees. Cook shrimp until golden brown. Serve with orange amaretto sauce.

SEASONED FLOUR

2 to 3 cups all-purpose flour
1 teaspoon salt
¼ teaspoon black ground pepper

Combine all ingredients. Store covered at room temperature until needed.

EGG WASH

3 whole eggs
3 tablespoons milk

Combine ingredients and refrigerate until needed.

ALMOND-SEASONED CRUMBS

2 cups slivered almonds, toasted

2 cups Italian bread crumbs (recipe below)

Place almonds into food processor and finely mince—about ⅛ inch in size. Be careful not to overprocess into a paste or flour. Place bread crumbs in a stainless steel mixing bowl. Add minced almonds and toss well. Store in covered plastic container at room temperature until needed.

ITALIAN BREAD CRUMBS

1¾ cups fine-grind bread crumbs

¼ teaspoon garlic powder

¼ teaspoon McCormick Italian seasoning

¼ teaspoon dried basil

¼ teaspoon ground black pepper

¼ teaspoon salt

¼ cup freshly grated Parmesan cheese

Combine all ingredients and mix well. Store at room temperature until needed.

ORANGE AMARETTO SAUCE

¼ cup Smuckers or Dickinson's orange marmalade

⅛ to ¼ cup Heinz cider vinegar, to taste

¼ cup Dijon mustard

½ cup amaretto

¼ cup freshly squeezed lemon juice

Combine ingredients in a large stainless steel bowl. Using a wire whisk mix until thoroughly incorporated. Place in plastic container. Store in refrigerator until needed.

C. JAMES KOCH

Chairman and CEO, Boston Beer Company

SAMUEL ADAMS BOSTON LAGER is a beer with a past. In 1977, while climbing Mt. McKinley as a mountaineering instructor with Outward Bound, C. James Koch unexpectedly stared that past squarely in the face when he came across an empty beer can at the top of the mountain. The experience stayed with him—nagged at him, really. His family had brewed beer in St. Louis since the 1870s, but the brewery had fallen on hard times in the 1960s and was closed by the time he was a teen. When he came across that empty beer can atop the mountain, he already had graduated from Harvard University and seemed destined for a stuffy career in business. Putting away his climbing gear, he returned to school and earned graduate degrees in business and law. Still, there was that beer can. After graduation he took a job with the Boston Consulting Group, where he worked with Fortune 500 companies. But the image of that beer can continued to linger. One day six years later, when he could stand it no longer, he rescued his family's beer recipe from his father's attic. The recipe was written out on a yellowed scrap of paper and hardly seemed the stuff of which dreams are made. But with the help of his father and several family friends, he created the Boston Beer Company and began bottling the family recipe under the label of Samuel Adams Boston Lager. In the beginning he literally took his product door-to-door in an effort to convince Boston-area bartenders of the product's worth.

Today, with 15 varieties on the market and sales of nearly $200 million a year, the Boston Beer Company is considered the top specialty beer producer in the United States.

Guest List

My wife, three daughters, son,
and my parents.

Menu

Gazpacho with shrimp,
served with Samuel Adams Golden Pilsner

Mixed greens with herbed orange vinaigrette,
served with Samuel Adams Boston Lager

Melegueta peppered Delmonico steak, pan-seared to a
perfect medium rare, in a Samuel Adams Cream Stout
mushroom pan sauce, served with parsleyed potatoes
and fiddlehead ferns,
served with Samuel Adams Boston Ale

Chocolate soufflé cake with Triple Bock whipped cream,
served with Samuel Adams Triple Bock

TRENT LOTT

United States Senator, Mississippi

WHEN SENATOR TRENT LOTT of Mississippi was named Senate Majority Leader in 1996, he became the first Mississippian to hold that powerful leadership post. In fact, his entire career has been marked by a series of political "firsts." Before his election to the Senate in 1988, he served in the House of Representatives, where he was elected Republican Whip, the second-ranking party leadership position. He was the first Southerner ever elected to that position, and he was reelected three times before moving on to the Senate, where he was chosen Senate Majority Whip one year before becoming Senate Majority Leader. He is the first person ever elected to the position of whip in both the Senate and the House of Representatives—and the first Southerner to serve in both posts. Many voters in his home state, where lemon icebox pie and barbecue reign supreme, believe the politically conservative son of a sharecropper someday will become the first Mississippian elected president.

Guest List

My beautiful wife, Tricia;
our son, Chet, and his wife, Diane;
our daughter, Tyler; and my mother
and father. This sounds like a
wonderful way to spend an evening,
especially my last supper.

Menu

Big plate of barbecue
French fries
Salad
Lemon icebox pie

Trent's Favorite Chocolate Candy

1 box Baker's semisweet chocolate, 8 squares

½ box Baker's unsweetened chocolate, 4 squares

1 can Eagle brand condensed milk

1 teaspoon vanilla extract

1 cup chopped pecan halves

¼ cup pecan halves

Melt chocolate squares over medium-low heat in the top of a double boiler, stirring constantly. Add condensed milk, vanilla, and chopped pecans. Stir well and drop by teaspoon onto waxed paper. Top with pecan halves. (The candy does not get real firm.) Keep in an airtight container to maintain freshness.

JOHN McCAIN

United States Senator, Arizona

For nearly two decades Republican John McCain has represented Arizona in Congress, first as a U.S. representative (1982–1986), and then as a U.S. senator (1986–present). In some respects he represents the last of a vanishing breed: Americans who devote their entire lives to public service.

In McCain's case, his public service began in the military. After graduating from the U.S. Naval Academy in 1958, he became an aviator and served for 22 years in the navy before retiring as a captain in 1981. His attraction to a military career came naturally: Both his father, John S. McCain Jr., and his grandfather, John S. McCain Sr., were admirals. McCain is one of a handful of baby boomer war heroes who have had an impact on Congress. In 1967 he was shot down over Hanoi and held as a prisoner of war in Vietnam for five and a half years. As a result of his wartime service, he received numerous medals, including the Silver Star, Bronze Star, Purple Heart, and Distinguished Flying Cross.

McCain, who serves on the Senate Armed Services Committee, signed on as a national security adviser to Bob Dole during his 1996 presidential campaign. In 1997 McCain was named one of *Time* magazine's "Top 25 Most Influential People in America." In recent years he has been mentioned as a possible presidential candidate. Apart from his long record of public service, McCain's single most distinguishing characteristic has been his positive relationship with the news media.

Arizona Baked Beans

1 teaspoon butter

1 medium onion, chopped

1 16-ounce can red kidney beans

1 16-ounce can B&M baked beans

1 cup ketchup

1 cup packed brown sugar

1 tablespoon vinegar

1 teaspoon French's yellow mustard

4 strips fried bacon, cooled and crumbled

Heat butter in a skillet and sauté chopped onion. In a large bowl, combine kidney beans, B&M baked beans, ketchup, brown sugar, vinegar, mustard, and crumbled bacon. After stirring enough to mix the ingredients, add the sautéed onion. Mix well.

Bake in a covered dish in a preheated 350 to 375-degree oven for 35 minutes, or until piping hot.

This dish is perfect with barbecued foods.

FRED THOMPSON

United States Senator, Tennessee

I F SENATOR FRED THOMPSON looks familiar, it may be because of his very high profile in the United States Senate, where he has represented Tennessee since 1994. Or it may be because of his stint in the early 1970s as minority counsel to the so-called Watergate committee investigating President Richard Nixon. Most likely, though, his familiarity derives from the 18 movies and 10 television shows in which he has appeared as an actor. Tall and lumbering, with a face that appears much more weather-worn than it actually is, he has the appearance of the no-nonsense sheriff from *Walking Tall* that you'd want to think twice about tangling with. His movie credits include *Die Hard 2* with Bruce Willis, *The Hunt for Red October* with Sean Connery, and *In the Line of Fire* with Clint Eastwood. His television credits include *China Beach*, *Roseanne*, and *Matlock*. Thompson began his legal career as an assistant U.S. attorney in the eastern district of Tennessee, where he earned a reputation as a tough prosecutor by winning convictions against a string of corrupt sheriffs and moonshiners. He began his political career in 1971 by serving as U.S. senator Howard Baker's campaign manager. In recent years the conservative Republican has been frequently mentioned as a presidential candidate. He makes his home in Nashville, where he has practiced law between his stints as a Hollywood actor. When asked for a last supper, he responded with a couple of recipes from his mother, Ruth Thompson, who is famous throughout Tennessee for her sweet and tasty coconut concoctions.

Menu

Ruth Thompson's fresh coconut cake
with fluffy white frosting

Ruth Thompson's
coconut cream pie

Ruth Thompson's Fresh Coconut Cake

WHITE CAKE

½ cup vegetable shortening

1¼ cups granulated sugar

2 cups sifted cake flour

2½ teaspoons baking powder

¼ teaspoon salt

1 cup milk

1 teaspoon vanilla extract

3 egg whites

1 fresh coconut

Cream shortening and sugar until fluffy. Sift flour, baking powder, and salt together three times. Then add milk, a little at a time, beating until smooth. Add vanilla extract. Beat egg whites into stiff peaks and gently fold into batter.

Bake in two greased-and-floured 8" or 9" cake pans in a preheated 350-degree oven for 30 minutes or until done. Let cool.

Open fresh coconut. Dribble coconut milk over each layer before frosting. Retain coconut meat.

FLUFFY WHITE FROSTING

1⅔ cups granulated sugar

½ cup water

¼ teaspoon cream of tartar

½ cup egg whites (3)

Reserved fresh coconut

In a pot, stir sugar, water, and cream of tartar over a low heat until sugar dissolves. Boil without stirring until syrup threads from spoon.

Meanwhile, beat egg whites until stiff. Add syrup gradually, beating constantly until cool enough to spread.

Frost top and sides of cake. Grate fresh coconut and sprinkle on top and sides.

Ruth Thompson's Coconut Cream Pie

2 whole eggs, separated

1¼ cups sugar

2 heaping teaspoons cornstarch

2 cups milk

2 teaspoons vanilla extract

1 can Baker's Angel Flake Coconut

1 baked pie shell

½ teaspoon cream of tartar

Beat yolks together lightly. Combine with 1 cup sugar, the cornstarch, milk, and 1 teaspoon vanilla extract and cook in a pan over a low heat, stirring constantly until mixture thickens. Add ½ can coconut. Spoon into baked pie shell.

Meanwhile, beat egg whites into stiff peaks and fold in ¼ cup sugar, 1 teaspoon vanilla extract, and cream of tartar. Spread meringue over the pie and sprinkle with remaining coconut. Lightly brown in oven.

GEORGE ZIMMER

CEO, The Men's Wearhouse

YOU KNOW HIM AS the ever-present Men's Wearhouse spokesman who ends every television commercial with the pledge, "I guarantee it!" What you probably don't know is that George Zimmer is the chief executive officer of a multimillion-dollar retail business that operates 375 stores in 39 states. Shortly after graduating from Washington University in St. Louis, Missouri, with a degree in economics, Zimmer founded the first Men's Wearhouse outlet in Houston, Texas, with a personal investment of only $7,000 in cash. Today The Men's Wearhouse has more than 5,000 employees and is publicly traded on the NASDAQ stock exchange. The secret to his success, he says, is to put people first and to unlock their individual potential. Therefore, he is fond of reminding people that he is in the people business, not the men's suit business. That philosophy has been transferred to his company's mission statement, which encourages the adoption of values that promote "a happy and healthy lifestyle" and the attainment of goals that encourage his employees to be "self-actualized people." About his last supper menu, he said: "I know it may not sound very appetizing, but it really hits the spot." Yes. He guarantees it!

Menu

Oatmeal with brown sugar and low-fat milk
Scrambled eggs

ARTS AND LETTERS

WRITERS LIKE FOOD as much as the next person, with the poundage of departed literary lions such as Thomas Wolfe and James Dickey attesting to that. But they are loathe to give anything away, especially if it is attached to a marketable idea. It's not that writers, by nature, are stingy. It's just that they tend to be collectors. They awake in the middle of the night and write down their dreams in the hopes they will someday provide them with a hook for a poem, novel, or short story, and they cannot enjoy a meal in a restaurant without searching their pockets for a scrap of paper on which to note the bizarre antics of the couple seated at the table across the room. Asking a writer for a recipe or list of menu items is like asking a stockbroker for free advice or a physician for a free exam.

If the first thing you don't want to ask a writer for is an idea, the second is for an opinion about anything even remotely associated with death. Writers are notoriously queasy about the subject. There are probably good reasons for that. Many professions deal with the physical manifestations of death on a regular basis—physicians, lawyers, embalmers, etc.—but only one profession requires its members, on a regular basis, to think about and describe the particulars of death and, by association, its possible spiritual extension. The first job requirement for a serious writer is to be able to empathize with the dead. Some find it easier than others.

So, as you can see, *Last Suppers* hit writers where it hurts the most. Those who responded to the author's queries have two things in common: First, all are doing quite well financially, thank you—Joe Eszterhas gets a zillion dollars per screenplay these days and Faye Kellerman couldn't write a book if she tried that didn't make the best-seller lists. Second, they apparently have made that all-important separate peace with death (Kellerman's spirituality is evident in her menu).

ROBERT C. ATKINS, M.D.

Diet Book Author,

Founder of the Atkins Center for Complementary Medicine

A LEADER IN THE FIELDS OF NATURAL MEDICINE and nutritional pharmacology, Dr. Robert Atkins became a best-selling author in 1972 with the publication of his book, *Dr. Atkins' Diet Revolution,* which has sold more than 10 million copies worldwide and has been translated into eight languages. It is one of only two diet books listed on the top 50 best-selling books of all time. His follow-up book, *Dr. Atkins' New Diet Revolution,* published in 1992, remained on *The New York Times* best-seller list for more than a year. His most recent book, *Dr. Atkins' Vita-Nutrient Solution,* advocates the use of nutrients as medical tools. Natural substances are at the core of Dr. Atkins' treatment philosophy. A practicing physician for more than 30 years, he is a strong advocate of the natural healing arts as a rational, effective alternative to pharmaceutical drugs and surgery for many debilitating illnesses. Through his writings and public appearances, he has brought national attention and credibility to complementary medicine as an effective medical approach. For his last supper Dr. Atkins chose a recipe from a book he coauthored with his wife, Veronica Atkins. The book, *Dr. Atkins' Quick and Easy New Diet Cookbook,* was published in 1997 as a companion to his previous books.

Grilled Lemon and Rosemary Lamb

5 tablespoons fresh lemon juice

½ cup olive oil

1 tablespoon fresh rosemary,
    or 1½ teaspoons dried rosemary

1 clove garlic, minced

2 teaspoons grated lemon zest

1 pound boneless lamb chops,
    cut into 1-inch cubes

Preheat the grill or broiler. Whisk together the lemon juice, olive oil, rosemary, garlic, and lemon zest in a bowl. Add the lamb and toss gently, making sure each piece is well coated. Cover and put in the refrigerator for 10 to 15 minutes. Thread the lamb onto skewers and grill or broil, turning once, for 12 minutes for medium. Serve immediately. Serves 2.

JAMES L. DICKERSON

Author of Last Suppers

W<small>HILE WRITING THIS BOOK</small>, the question most often asked of me by the celebrities themselves was, "So, what are you having for your last supper?" It was a fair question and I toyed with a variety of tasty possibilities. In the end I took the route followed by Coach Ditka and others in this book: I reverted to my childhood. My menu, with the exception of the Chianti (which is another story entirely), was compiled from the childhood meal that consoled me when my dog Ruff disappeared, when my 12-year-old heart was broken by a brown-eyed girl who was the shining star of the sixth grade, and when my pet groundhogs escaped and terrorized my hometown with their snappish antics. The ultimate last supper, I have concluded, is one that allows you to go out of this world with some semblance of childhood memory. Besides, there is always the possibility that "mother knows best."

Guest List

William Faulkner

Martin Luther King

Ernest Hemingway

Stonewall Jackson

Eudora Welty

Howling Wolf

Marilyn Monroe

Calista Flockhart

Claudia Schiffer

The Dixie Chicks

Pierre Elliott Trudeau

Shania Twain

Rhonda Shear

Menu

Baked potato

Green salad

Bottle of cheap chianti wine (must be in basket)

Frozen French pastry

Entertainment

The Amazing Kreskin
(with David Letterman as his assistant)

Louis Armstrong

A hoochie-coochie dancer named Julee who found God in the
emergency room of a Memphis hospital

Hot Tamale Pie
(Juanita Caldwell's original recipe)

1 tablespoon oil
1 large onion, chopped
1½ pounds ground beef
2 cans condensed tomato soup
1 teaspoon salt
¼ teaspoon black pepper
3 heaping tablespoons chili powder
¾ cup chopped black olives
¾ cup whole kernel corn

Heat oil in a large skillet and brown onion and meat. Add remaining ingredients and stir for a few minutes until heated through. Pour in greased casserole, cover, and bake in a preheated 325-degree oven for 1½ hours.

TOPPING

¾ cup self-rising corn meal
½ stick margarine, room temperature
1 egg
¼ teaspoon baking soda
Enough buttermilk to make soft batter

Mix together topping ingredients. Add topping to mixture and return to oven, uncovered, for about 25 minutes. Serve.

Frozen French Pastry

(Juanita Caldwell's original recipe)

1⅓ sticks margarine or butter

4 whole eggs, beaten

1 pound box powdered sugar

1 box vanilla wafers

1 cup chopped nuts

1 large container
  frozen strawberries

1 large can crushed pineapple,
  drained and chilled

2 half pints whipped cream

Make praline syrup by combining 1 stick of margarine, eggs, and powdered sugar in a double boiler. Cook uncovered for 1½ hours. Stir occasionally.

Meanwhile, crush vanilla wafers and nuts and ⅓ stick melted margarine. Mix together and spread in bottom of a 9"x12" container; reserve a few crumbs to sprinkle on top. Pour syrup over crumbs, cover tightly, and place in freezer to chill.

Fold frozen strawberries and crushed pineapple into whipped cream. Spoon over syrup layer. Sprinkle with remaining crumbs and freeze. Slice in squares and serve.

JOE ESZTERHAS

Screenwriter

J OE ESZTERHAS is one of the most successful and talked-about screenwriters in cinema history. His 1992 psychological thriller, *Basic Instinct*, starring Sharon Stone and Michael Douglas, grossed nearly $120 million domestically and launched Stone's career as an A-list movie actress. Born in Csakanydoroszlo, Hungary, Eszterhas came to the United States when he was 6 years old. After a brief career as a newspaper and magazine journalist—he did a stint with *Rolling Stone* magazine and unearthed details of the infamous My Lai massacre while he was working as a reporter for the Cleveland *Plain Dealer*—he authored a book, *Charlie Simpson's Apocalypse*, and then gravitated to Hollywood, where he found his niche as a screenwriter. He has written 17 films to date, including *Jagged Edge*, *Showgirls*, *Telling Lies in America*, and *Burn Hollywood Burn*. He lives in Malibu, California, with his wife, Naomi, and three young sons.

Menu

One loaf of very fresh sourdough bread

One bottle of very dry, very cold French or
California white wine

Begin meal with very sharp
Canadian cheddar cheese

Follow with a salad of thinly sliced cucumbers, no dressing

Main Course

Hungarian chicken paprika, with dumplings

Dessert

Naomi's oatmeal-raisin cookies

FAYE KELLERMAN

Author

AT ONE END OF FAYE KELLERMAN'S Los Angeles home is an office, in which she crafts the intricate plots and psychological twists and turns of her novels, most of which feature her favorite protagonists, Rina Lazurus and Peter Decker. At the other end of her home is an office usually occupied by her husband, author Jonathan Kellerman, a former child psychologist who matches his wife's literary output with novels of his own. It is not uncommon for the Kellermans to have competing novels on the best-seller list, if not at the same time, certainly within a few months of each other. Despite their friendly, in-house literary competition, the Kellermans obviously have had time for more traditional marital pursuits, such as the conception, care, and nurturing of their four children. One of the aspects of Faye Kellerman's work that makes it distinctive is the inclusion of characters who are identified as Orthodox Jews. The reason is that both Faye and Jonathan Kellerman are modern Orthodox Jews who have maintained, fiercely at times, their religious identity in a Los Angeles community not necessarily known for its religious diversity or specificity. Not surprising, Faye Kellerman's last supper is an expression of her Jewish heritage. Her most recent best-seller is *Moon Music*, in which detective Romulus Poe's investigation of a showgirl's murder uncovers threads of Las Vegas's sordid past. Other novels include *Ritual Bath* and *Justice*.

Guest List

My husband, Jonathan, and my children—
Jesse, Rachel, Ilana, Aliza

My mother and brothers and their families

Jonathan's family
(whoever would want to come)

Moshe Rabbenu (Moses), our rabbi,
and family

Aaron, Moses's brother,
and family

Miriam, Moses's sister,
and family

Abraham and Sarah

Isaac and Rebekkah

Jacob and Rachel and Leah,
plus handmaidens

The 12 sons of Jacob and wives and children

You'll need a long, long table for this one.
Prepare to stay up all night and then some.

Menu

I am a traditional Jew, so my last supper would have to be a traditional seder. All of the items not only would be kosher but would be kosher for Passover as well. The menu would go as follows:

Chicken broth with matzoh ball and beef bone

Individual round molded rings of fish layered in the following manner: ground, spiced whitefish on the bottom, a tier of chopped spinach, a layer of peppered salmon, and then grated carrots, topped with whitefish and served with horseradish sauce

A fresh garden salad with raspberry vinaigrette

The entrée would be rib roast, medium rare, served with rosemary/paprika potatoes and fresh asparagus topped with hollandaise sauce

A trio of sorbets—raspberry, tangerine, and peach—served with a waffle cookie

Ended, of course, with the ritual *afikomen*

CARL REINER
Comedian / Actor / Writer / Director

W HEN CARL REINER began his television career in the 1950s on Sid Caesar's *Your Show of Shows*, the medium was in its infancy. The skits he wrote and costarred in with Caesar and writing partner Mel Brooks were groundbreaking and set the stage for the later success of cutting-edge shows such as *Saturday Night Live*. In the 1960s Reiner wrote, produced, and directed the award-winning *Dick Van Dyke Show*, in which he also played the role of Van Dyke's boss, Alan Brady. In the 1970s he directed two of the decade's most successful films, *Oh God!*, starring George Burns, and *The Jerk*, starring Steve Martin. Shadowing the success of his television shows and films have been a series of successful comedy albums he cowrote and corecorded with Mel Brooks entitled *The 2000 Year Old Man*. The five albums were all nominated for Grammys, including the most recent, *The 2000 Year Old Man in the Year 2000*. Most students of television consider Reiner the most creative and dominant figure yet to emerge from the medium. His son, Rob Reiner, hasn't done half bad either.

Potlejel

1 firm, lightweight eggplant

1 whole lemon

3 tablespoons olive oil

Salt substitute, to taste

Pepper, to taste

1 onion, finely chopped

Choose a firm but lightweight eggplant. Place directly on high gas burner; do not use saucer or pot. Turn regularly for 5 to 6 minutes until charred and tender. With a long fork remove eggplant from burner and place under cold tap water for easier peeling. Peel charred skin.

Put peeled eggplant on large plate and slice open. Squeeze lemon on eggplant to keep it from turning brown. Tilt plate and spoon off bitter juices. Mash coarsely with wooden spoon. Add olive oil, salt substitute, and pepper to taste. Store in glass jar in refrigerator until ready to serve.

Before serving, mix in onions. Can be used as a dip or hors d'oeuvre on crackers or on cucumber slices.

SPORTS

Sports figures are among America's most accessible celebrities. Even so, readers will notice an imbalance in this section, with the most space devoted to professional golfers. That's because every golfer contacted, with one or two exceptions, responded with recipes or lists of menu items. Football players came in second, with baseball and basketball players nowhere in sight. Golfers probably topped the list because they spend their careers on playing fields where their fans are only a stone's throw away. When golfers go to work, they actually converse with their fans on a daily basis. Baseball and basketball players, by contrast, often seem downright fan unfriendly. The only time they confront their fans is usually in the parking lot amid a mad dash for their limos. Of the NASCAR drivers contacted, only John Andretti responded with a last supper. As it turns out, most NASCAR drivers are superstitious about anything related to death. "These guys put their lives on the line day after day on the track," explained one publicist, who said he was afraid to ask his boss for a recipe. "Not many of them are gonna want to think about their last supper."

"John Andretti did!"

"No kidding," responded the publicist, a soft whistle expressing his admiration.

JOHN ANDRETTI

Race Car Driver

JOHN ANDRETTI began his racing career at the tender age of 9. With a name like Andretti—John's father, Aldo, is Mario's twin brother—no one in his family was surprised. The fact that John's first race car was a go-cart hardly mattered. He had racing in his blood, and it was only a matter of time before he found his way to the souped-up NASCAR machines that had made his uncle famous. After studying at Andre Pillette's driving school at Zolder, Belgium, John began open-wheel road racing at the age of 16. From there he worked his way up the circuit, driving an assortment of stock cars and sprint cars. In 1994 he became the first driver ever to compete in the Indianapolis 500 and the Charlotte 600 on the same day. By 1997 he had captured his first Winston Cup trophy with a win in the Pepsi 400 at Daytona. The following year the 34-year-old racer chalked up 15 top 10 wins and earned in excess of $3 million, making him one of the emerging bright stars of the NASCAR circuit.

Guest List

My wife, Nancy, and my two children, Jarett and Olivia. To me, there is no one more special, and my last moments should be spent with them. I just could not put any other person in front of these three people. Also, since this is the "last" day, I will probably, if I am fortunate enough to go to heaven myself, meet all of the individuals that I have ever had a desire to meet.

Menu

Nonna Rina's soup with soup balls

Nonna Rina's gnocchi with brown sauce

Nonna Rina's peas

Nonna Rina's spinach

Nonna Rina's sweet potatoes

Granny Stofflet's baked corn

Mom's store-bought dinner rolls
(which are always late and always burned)

Dessert

Nonna Rina's almond cake with icing

Nonna Rina's Soup

4 quarts water

2 whole carrots

16 packets George Washington
Golden Seasoning and Broth Mix

2 whole celery tops

1 unpeeled onion

1 or 2 beef shanks or soup bone

Simmer all ingredients for 2 hours, skimming off brown froth that rises to top. When cooked pour through colander, reserving the broth. Store cooled broth in refrigerator. When ready to serve, you can add soup balls and egg pastina.

SOUP BALLS

2 whole eggs

8 tablespoons butter,
room temperature

Parmesan cheese (small amount)

1 Cup Cream of Wheat

Beat eggs and add to butter; mix together. Add cheese and mix. Then add Cream of Wheat. Mix well and form into very small balls. Cook 20 minutes in soup broth or until done. Broth should be at a medium boil.

Nonna Rina's Gnocchi

4 pounds potatoes

2 tablespoons salt

1 stick butter

2 beaten eggs

4 cups flour

Parmesan cheese

Cook potatoes with jackets on in salted water until done. Peel and mash potatoes while hot. Place butter in center of hot mashed potatoes. Once butter has melted—about 5 to 10 minutes—mix potatoes thoroughly. Cover with dish towel and allow to cool. Make a small well in center of potatoes and pour in eggs and mix well. Gradually add flour. Knead well to form dough. Separate mixture into four equal parts. Sprinkle each with a little flour. Form each portion into a roll the thickness of a sausage. Slice in pieces slightly thicker than a half inch. Gently roll each piece on a flat grader, slightly curling each piece. Pieces should resemble macaroni shells. Cook in 4 quarts boiling, salted water (cook about one third of total amount at a time) for about 20 to 30 seconds. Gnocchi will rise to top of boiling water when done. Gently scoop out with a slotted spoon as they rise to top. Serve with brown sauce. Sprinkle with Parmesan cheese.

BROWN SAUCE

3 tablespoons butter or margarine

1 large onion, diced

2 pounds cubed beef

1 teaspoon Accent

Salt and pepper, to taste

½ tablespoon nutmeg

2 tablespoons oil

1 tablespoon flour

1 8-ounce can tomato sauce

Heat butter in a pot and sauté onion until it becomes translucent. Add meat, Accent, salt, pepper, and nutmeg. Slowly fry meat until brown. While meat is browning in a separate small frying pan, heat oil. Once oil is hot, stir in flour to make a gravy paste. Add the paste to meat. Next add tomato sauce and stir. Add just enough water to cover the meat. Simmer for at least 1½ hours. Transfer to a crock pot and simmer overnight with the lid off.

Nonna Rina's Peas

1 stick butter or margarine

2 teaspoons minced garlic

2 tablespoons parsley flakes

1 small bag frozen peas

Accent to taste

Melt butter in frying pan. Add garlic and parsley flakes. Add frozen peas and Accent. Sauté for 10 to 15 minutes.

Nonna Rina's Spinach

4 10-ounce boxes of frozen spinach

Salt and pepper, to taste

Accent to taste

1 stick butter or margarine

4 heaping tablespoons
  plain bread crumbs

Place spinach in a pot with a little water. Add salt, pepper, and Accent. Boil until fully thawed. Drain spinach thoroughly in a colander. Melt butter in a large frying pan, then add bread crumbs. Mix spinach with bread crumbs and serve.

Nonna Rina's Sweet Potatoes

2 sticks butter or margarine

2 cups brown sugar

2 large cans sweet potatoes or yams, drained and mashed

1 can crushed pineapple

Melt butter or margarine in a large frying pan, and add brown sugar. Stir. Add drained and mashed sweet potatoes. Stir and add undrained pineapple. Simmer on low heat for 30 minutes.

Granny Stofflet's Baked Corn

2 tablespoons flour

½ teaspoon salt

½ teaspoon sugar

¼ teaspoon pepper

1 egg

1 can crushed corn

¼ cup milk

1 tablespoon butter

Combine all ingredients in baking dish and bake in a preheated 350 degree oven for 1 hour. For family get-togethers, make four times the amount.

Nonna Rina's Almond Cake

14 eggs

2 cups sugar

2 teaspoons pure lemon extract

5 cups ground almonds

5 teaspoons imitation rum flavor

Butter to coat baking pans

Flour to coat baking pans

4 squares grated sweet chocolate

Separate eggs. Beat egg yolks, sugar, and lemon together until smooth. Beat egg whites until peaks are soft, and then gently fold egg whites into yolk mixture. Slowly add nuts and rum. Bake in four buttered-and-floured 9" pans in a preheated 325-degree oven for 15 minutes. Then turn the oven to 350 degrees and bake until golden brown—about 10 minutes. Finish at 325 degrees for about 5 minutes. The total baking time should be about 30 minutes. Turn off oven, open the door, and let the cake rest for 5 minutes before removing. Meanwhile, melt chocolate in a makeshift double boiler. When the cakes have cooled, remove from pans. Spread melted chocolate between layers and stack.

ICING

¾ cup sweet butter

2 eggs, separated

¾ cup sugar

2 ounces grated sweet chocolate

Cream butter until smooth. Mix egg yolks and sugar until smooth; then add to butter. Beat egg whites to soft peaks, and fold into yolk mixture. Gently stir in grated chocolate. Frost cake.

BOBBY BOWDEN

Coach, Florida State University Seminoles

BOBBY BOWDEN is the second-highest-paid coach in college football. The reason, as sportswriters are fond of pointing out, can be found in the stats: Florida State University is one of the winningest teams in college football history. In 23 years at Florida State, Bowden has seen his teams chalk up more than 200 victories and 20 bowl game appearances. Florida State is the only school to finish among the Associated Press Top Four for 12 consecutive seasons, which translates to 12 straight seasons of 10 or more wins. "I just love to coach," Bowden says. "That may sound simple, but I think sometimes people like the things that go around coaching and not the actual job. I have always gotten my greatest pleasure out of breaking down film, learning about opponents and yourself, then implementing a game plan to take advantage of your strengths and their weaknesses. I love to take a group of young men in the late summer and mold them into a team."

Bowden's Easy Chocolate Cake

CAKE

2 sticks butter

4 tablespoons cocoa

1 cup water

2 cups all-purpose, unsifted flour

2 cups sugar

2 whole eggs, beaten together lightly

1 teaspoon baking soda

1 cup sour cream

Heat butter, cocoa, and water in large pan over moderate heat. Remove from heat. Add flour and sugar, and blend until fairly smooth. Add eggs, baking soda, and sour cream and blend until smooth. Pour in a greased 9" x 12" pan. Bake in a preheated 350-degree oven for approximately 30 to 35 minutes. Cool and frost.

FROSTING

1 stick butter

4 tablespoons cocoa

4 tablespoons milk

1 pound powdered sugar

1 teaspoon vanilla extract

1 cup chopped nuts

To make the frosting, melt butter in a pan, add cocoa and milk, and blend together. Add powdered sugar and vanilla. Blend well. Stir in nuts. Pour frosting over cooled cake.

MIKE DITKA

Professional Football Coach

WHEN MIKE DITKA began his football career in 1961, he did so with a bang by being named the National Football League's "Rookie of the Year." Over an 11-year career as a tight end for the Chicago Bears, Philadelphia Eagles, and Dallas Cowboys, he ran up an impressive record of 427 catches for 5,812 yards and 43 touchdowns. Ditka was named to the Pro Bowl five times. When he left the playing field in 1972, it appeared, for a time, that he was going to fade away, as so many professional athletes before him had done. But it just wasn't in his nature to turn his back on football.

In 1982 he became the coach of the Chicago Bears, a position he held until 1992, when he left the Bears with an overall record of 112 wins and 68 losses. In 1986 he guided the team to a lopsided victory over New England in Super Bowl XX. It was during his tenure as the head coach of the Bears that he was elected to the Hall of Fame, in 1988. He is one of only two men in NFL history to win Super Bowl rings as a player, assistant coach, and head coach.

In 1997, after an absence of five years, during which time he delivered motivational speeches and worked as a studio analyst for NBC Sports, Ditka returned to football as the head coach of the New Orleans Saints. "I want to create a greater sense of pride in this organization," he said of the Saints, who in their 31-year franchise history had never won a playoff game. "It won't come easy. Nothing good in this life ever does."

Halupka

(pigs-in-a-blanket)

When I was a kid growing up in Pennsylvania, my mother, Charlotte, cooked a dish called Halupka, or pigs-in-a-blanket. It was a combination of rice, veal, beef, and pork, all ground up and put into a cabbage roll. She made a red sauce with it that was great, not just on the Halupka, but on mashed potatoes and things like that. The recipe was very involved. Everything depended on how many you made it for. She would make it in one of those big roasting pans you cook turkeys in, and it would be full. It's a delicious dish. It's like the Greek dish, although they use only one form of meat. My mother did it the right way, with veal and pork. If I had only one meal left, it would be her Halupka.

JOHN ELWAY

Quarterback, Denver Broncos

WHEN JOHN ELWAY led the Denver Broncos to their first Super Bowl win by defeating the Green Bay Packers, 31–24, he made it look remarkably easy. Lost in the excitement of the day was the fact that he had labored for 14 arduous years to savor that moment. Acquired in a 1983 trade with the then-Baltimore Colts, Elway had little experience in professional football when he reported to the Broncos training camp. No one was sure what to expect of the rookie quarterback. He looked promising, but so do most rookies. Elway went on to break every passing record imaginable for the Denver franchise and to earn himself a certain place in the Football Hall of Fame in Canton, Ohio. Today he is widely regarded as one of the top quarterbacks ever to play the game.

Hamburger Soup

2 tablespoons butter

1 to 2 medium onions, chopped

1 clove garlic, minced

2 to 3 pounds ground beef

3 cans beef stock

1 medium can tomato sauce

1 large can of Rotel diced tomatoes and green chilies

1 cup diced raw potatoes with skins on

1 cup diced carrots

1 cup diced celery

1 can French-style green beans

1 cup dry red wine

1 tablespoon parsley

½ teaspoon basil

Salt and pepper, to taste

In a large pot, melt butter and sauté onions and minced garlic. Remove onions and garlic from pot, set aside, and fry ground beef. Drain grease. Add all ingredients to beef. Bring to a boil, reduce to a simmer, and cook until veggies are done. Season to taste. Serve with warm bread.

CAMMI GRANATO

Olympic Gold Medalist/Women's Ice Hockey

"OTHER PEOPLE WERE [always] putting limitations on me—'you're a girl, you can't play hockey,'" Cammi Granato told *Rolling Stone* magazine for its "1998 Sports Hall of Fame" feature. "But I didn't listen. It pushed me." For evidence of that you need look no further than the 1998 Winter Olympics in Nagano, Japan, where the 1998 United States Women's Ice Hockey Team shocked the world by capturing the Gold Medal. As team captain Granato emerged from the Olympics as sort of the Michael Jordan of women's hockey. Already known as the all-time scoring leader in the history of the United States Women's Ice Hockey program, she boosted the visibility of the sport by appearing on news and talk shows such as the *Late Show with David Letterman*, *Live with Regis and Kathy Lee*, and *Good Morning America*. A recent survey by the *Sports Business Daily* found the winsome hockey pro to be among the top 20 most marketable female athletes in the world, a fact made evident by a string of advertising campaigns for AT&T, Nike, and Chevrolet. Granato's skills on the ice are matched by her talents as a motivational speaker. She has appeared before Congress and a number of corporate audiences, and she has worked as a color analyst for the National Hockey League's Los Angeles Kings on KRLA-AM radio.

Ginger Chicken & Vegetable Stir Fry

Fresh mushrooms

Carrots

Broccoli

Sugar snap peas

1 tablespoon light oil

2 small chicken breasts, cut up

Finely chopped ginger, to taste

Teriyaki sauce, optional

Cooked white rice

Chop up vegetables. Heat oil in a wok and fry chicken with finely chopped ginger, stirring constantly. After chicken is cooked, toss in vegetables, stirring constantly for 2 to 3 minutes more. You can add teriyaki sauce or other desired seasoning. Serve over white rice

FOR DESSERT

Blueberries, raspberries, and strawberries mixed with vanilla yogurt. Top with sprinkled wheat germ and enjoy.

HALE IRWIN
Professional Golfer

With 16 senior tournaments over the past two years and earnings of nearly $3 million last year, Hale Irwin is one of the most active and successful players on the Senior PGA Tour. Last year he capped the season with seven wins. The previous year he had nine victories and tied Peter Thomson's 1985 record for the most wins in one season. You would think that any golfer capable of running up numbers like that must have been born with a single-minded devotion to the sport. Not necessarily so. As a student at the University of Colorado, Irwin was torn between golf and football—he was the 1967 NCAA Champion and was a two-time Big Eight selection as a football defensive back. Obviously, golf won out in the end, but for a while Irwin was torn over the direction he wanted his life to take. That dual interest in football and golf has extended to his family. His son, Steve, is pursuing a career as a professional golfer, and his nephew Heath is an offensive lineman with the New England Patriots. Today, Hale Irwin may be the only player on the Senior PGA Tour capable of blitzing the final hole and sacking his caddie.

Hale's Favorite Pecan Pie

3 whole eggs

½ cup sugar

Pinch salt

1 teaspoon vanilla extract

1 cup dark Karo syrup

3 tablespoons butter, melted, not hot

1¾ cups whole pecans

1 9" pie crust, unbaked

Beat eggs with fork. Add sugar, salt, vanilla, Karo syrup, butter, and pecans and mix well. Pour into pie shell and bake for 30 minutes in a preheated 350-degree oven. Don't bake more than 45 minutes. Depending upon how hot your oven gets, you may want to bake this closer to the bottom. Serve with sweetened whipped cream or vanilla ice cream.

JACK NICKLAUS
Professional Golfer

I F YOU'VE EVER WONDERED what went through golf legend Jack Nicklaus's mind as he lined up a big-money putt or put the final touches on a mind-boggling, zillion-under-par win at the Masters in Augusta, you might be justified in assuming—and the word *might* is used with more than a little caution—that he had his mind on a slice of his wife's delicious, old-fashioned Italian cream cake. That's my story, and I'm sticking to it.

When Nicklaus was first approached about submitting a last supper menu or recipe for this book, he pondered all the possibilities and then determined that the task offered way too many options. He couldn't pick just one menu.

"It would change too many times," he says.

Coming to Nicklaus's rescue was his wife, Barbara, who sized up that most difficult shot and offered her suggestion for a sure-fire culinary hole in one: her own recipe for Italian cream cake. It's what she knows Jack would want on his last-supper menu. "Jack loves it," she says. "Enjoy!"

Italian Cream Cake

2 cups sugar

½ cup butter

½ cup solid vegetable shortening

5 eggs, separated

1 teaspoon baking soda

1 cup buttermilk

2 cups flour

½ teaspoon salt

1 tablespoon vanilla extract

1 cup coconut

1 cup chopped pecans

Cream sugar, butter, and shortening together. Add egg yolks one at a time, beating well after each addition. Stir soda into buttermilk and let sit 10 minutes. Beat egg whites until stiff. Set aside. Sift flour and salt together. Add alternately with buttermilk to sugar and butter mixture. Add vanilla, coconut, and pecans. Fold in egg whites. Pour batter into three greased and floured 9" cake pans. Bake in a preheated 325-degree oven for 35 minutes.

CREAM

8 ounces cream cheese

½ cup butter

1 one-pound box of
   10X confectioners' sugar

1 teaspoon vanilla extract

Combine all ingredients. Spread between layers and on outside of cake. Decorate the top of cake with pecan halves and a little flaked coconut.

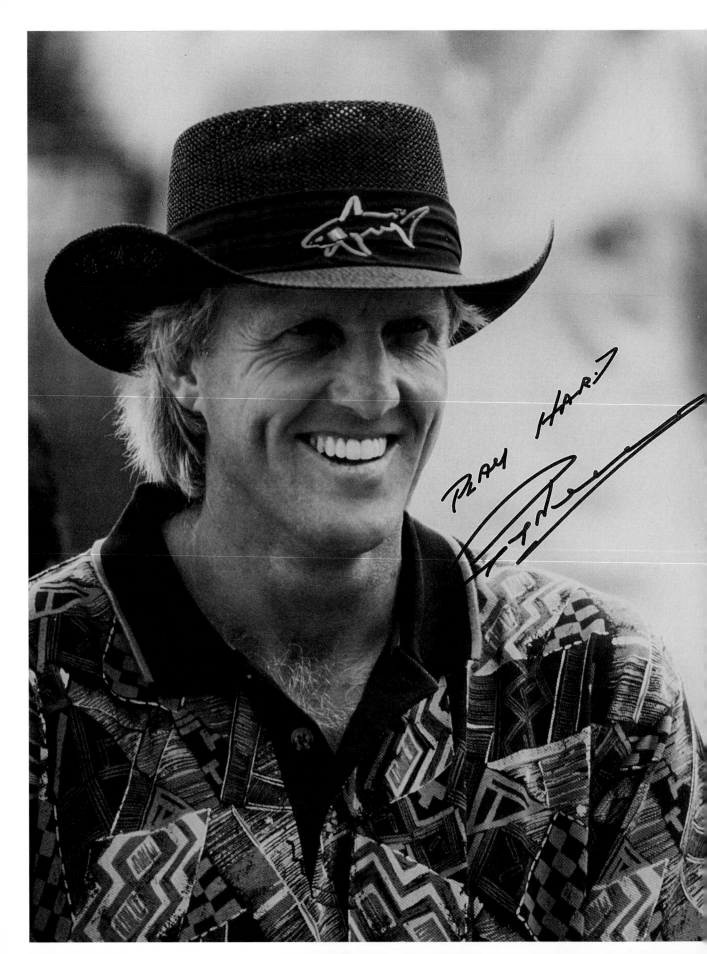

PLAY HARD

GREG NORMAN

Professional Golfer

For 20 years, Australian-born Greg Norman has been one of the world's most colorful golfers. A winner of two British opens and numerous world titles, he has cut back in recent years on his participation in the world tour and focused on his many business interests, which include a yacht company, a golf-course design firm, sportswear, restaurants, and a successful instructional video titled *One on One with Greg Norman*. In 1997, with earnings of $37 million (Australian) he topped *Business Review Weekly's* survey of Australia's richest sportsmen. In 1998, despite shoulder surgery earlier in the year, he helped the Internationals team defeat the United States in the Presidents Cup but lost by one hole to Tiger Woods in the singles play. Asked if he was disappointed by that loss, he said, "I don't get disappointed if somebody beat me because they were better on that day." Although Norman currently lives in Florida, he maintains close ties with his native country and has expressed a desire to return there someday to live and perhaps enjoy his last supper.

Australian Meat Pie

1 ounce butter or margarine

2 small onions, finely chopped

2 pounds chopped sirloin

2 tablespoons plain flour

2½ cups beef bouillon or stock

1 teaspoon dried thyme

2 tablespoons Worcestershire sauce

¼ cup chopped parsley

Pinch nutmeg

Salt and pepper, to taste

1 pie crust, top and bottom, unbaked

Butter for pie pan

1 egg, slightly beaten

Melt butter in a saucepan. Add onions and fry over medium heat until soft. Add beef and fry, pressing down with fork until beef is browned. Drain. Sprinkle flour over beef, stir, and continue cooking for two more minutes. Remove pan from heat. Gradually add stock and stir. Return pan to the heat and stir constantly until mixture boils and thickens. Add thyme, Worcestershire sauce, parsley, nutmeg, salt, and pepper. Cover pan and simmer over a low heat for 30 minutes.

Place pie shell in a buttered pie pan and prick the base of the shell several times with a fork. Using a sharp knife, trim off excess pastry. Spoon filling in. Brush around edge with beaten egg. Top with pastry, pressing edges together. Cut a hole in center of pie. Brush with remaining egg. Bake in a preheated 400-degree oven for 25 minutes or until crust is golden brown. Serves 4 or 5.

ARNOLD PALMER
Professional Golfer

To many people the name Arnold Palmer is synonymous with golf. Certainly, he is the sport's first superstar. Born in 1929 in Latrobe, Pennsylvania, he began his championship career with a win in the 1955 Canadian Open and went on to amass 92 championships, including 61 victories on the U.S. PGA Tour. His hottest period was in the early 1960s, when he landed 29 of his titles and collected $400,000 in earnings. That figure sounds low by today's standards; Tiger Woods collected $486,000 for his victory in the 1997 Masters. But in the early 1960s it was a substantial amount and established Palmer as a role model for succeeding generations of golfers. Associated Press writers voted him the "Athlete of the Year" for the entire decade of the 1960s. In recent years he has written numerous best-selling books and videos and devoted a great deal of time to charitable causes. Today Palmer serves as president of Arnold Palmer Enterprises and owner of the Latrobe Country Club. He continues to reside in Latrobe during the summer months, but prefers to winter in Orlando, Florida, where he has established a variety of business interests.

Sugared Bacon Strips

½ to 1 pound bacon
1 cup brown sugar

Roll or pat or shake raw bacon in brown sugar and place strips on any flat pan with sides. Bake in a slow oven—275 to 300 degrees—for about 25 to 30 minutes until dark brown. You may turn over once with pincers or tongs. When bacon appears well done, remove with tongs and drain on brown paper thoroughly; grocery bags are good for that. As it cools the bacon will harden and can be broken into smaller pieces or served whole. This tedious chore can be done earlier in the day and the bacon stored in aluminum foil and reheated to serve.

STEVE SPURRIER

Coach, University of Florida Gators

WITH A SALARY THAT APPROACHES $2 million a year, Steve Spurrier is the highest-paid college football coach in the country. The reasons are not hard to understand. Before his arrival as head coach in 1990, no Florida team had won a Southeastern Conference championship in 56 years. In his nine years at the university, the Gators have won a national title and posted 66 wins and nine losses in conference games. He is the only major collegiate coach in the 20th century to win more than 90 games in his first nine years at a school. Spurrier was hardly an unknown at Florida when he accepted a coaching position there. As a student at the University of Florida in the mid-1960s, he led the Gators to winning seasons with his skills as a quarterback. In 1966 he was awarded the Heisman Trophy. The following year he was a first-round draft choice of the San Francisco 49ers. In 1997 Spurrier received praise from women's groups by donating $50,000 to the University of Florida's women's athletic program.

Beef Bar-B-Q Sandwiches

6-pounds boneless sirloin steak

3 ounces Liquid Smoke
3 garlic cloves, chopped
Pepper, to taste
Onion salt, to taste
Garlic salt, to taste
Meat tenderizer
1 cup Worcestershire sauce

14 ounces ketchup
12 ounces chili sauce
⅓ cup mustard
1½ cups brown sugar
2 tablespoons pepper
1½ cups wine vinegar
1 cup lemon juice
½ cup thick steak sauce
Tabasco sauce, to taste
¼ tablespoon soy sauce
1 tablespoon salad oil
1 can beer
Minced garlic, to taste

MARINADE

Combine all ingredients and set aside until needed.

Marinate boneless sirloin steak for 24 to 48 hours in the refrigerator. Preheat oven to 275 degrees. Cook boneless sirloin for five hours in a covered container. Refrigerate to cool. Slice right before serving to avoid dryness. Serve on good sandwich rolls with barbecue sauce—or horse-radish, lettuce, tomato, and mayonnaise.

BARBECUE SAUCE

Mix ingredients together and apply to cooked meat.

REGGIE WHITE
Defensive End, Green Bay Packers

THEY DON'T COME MUCH BIGGER than Reggie White. The 6-foot-5-inch, 300-pound defensive end for the Green Bay Packers has broken all the records in his 13-year professional football career—750 career tackles and 299 assisted tackles—and focused a bit of excitement on a group of players who traditionally have been ignored for their work in the trenches: defensive linemen. Today he is one of the most recognizable and beloved players in the game, and his soup commercials have become minor classics. Off the field the outspoken White, who resigned from football in 1999, has generated controversy for his opinions on racial and ethnic differences, but he has maintained good humor throughout it all and left his critics to sort it out for themselves. White played his college football at the University of Tennessee in Knoxville and has maintained close ties to that community since he was drafted into the National Football League in 1985. Whether it had any bearing on his choice of a last supper is unknown, but he mailed in his recipe for scrambled eggs Florentine on December 20, the day after his 37th birthday.

Scrambled Eggs Florentine

1 whole egg
6 large egg whites
2 teaspoons butter
3 tablespoons chopped onion
3 tablespoons chopped mushrooms
1⅓ cups cooked spinach
2 ounces low-fat cheese

Beat eggs and set aside. Melt butter in a frying pan. Add chopped onion and mushrooms. Cook for a few minutes or until mushrooms give up their water. Slowly add cooked spinach and low-fat cheese. Add eggs. Cook until done.

CHEFS

WHAT'S A BOOK OF CELEBRITY last meals without the input of celebrity chefs? To weed out the culinary clunkers, I compiled a list of the finest chefs in America. That list was longer than I expected, for one of the unheralded changes of the past decade has been America's growing fascination with all things related to food and its expert preparation. For nominees, I looked to the experts, the food and restaurant writers and editors who regularly compile lists on the best and brightest of the profession. Believe it or not, there are people who spend their days and nights evaluating, analyzing, and partaking of the work product of this country's chefs.

After reviewing the work history and reputations of dozens of chefs, I put together what I feel is an ideal list. I'm confident that the culinary experts featured in this book—Todd English, Nora Pouillon, Daniel Boulud, Roland Passot, Tom Douglas, Stephan Pyles, Mario Ferrari, and Norman Van Aken—are among the top 10 chefs in America. All have won awards, made "best of" lists, or published award-winning cookbooks. All are true geniuses at the art of culinary expression.

Sadly, none sent in actual samples of their work.

DANIEL BOULUD

Restaurant Daniel and Café Boulud: New York, New York

Daniel Boulud is one of New York City's premier chefs. He is the owner of two restaurants—Restaurant Daniel and Café Boulud—and the co-owner of a third, Payard Patisserie & Bistro. The author of a cookbook, *Cooking with Daniel Boulud*, he writes a bimonthly column, "Daniel's Dish," which appears in *Elle Decor* magazine. Since opening his heralded Restaurant Daniel in 1993, he and his restaurant have garnered countless honors for the creativity of his French cuisine. The *International Herald Tribune* once described Restaurant Daniel as "one of the 10 best in the world." *The New York Times* consistently has given the restaurant four-star ratings. In 1998 Boulud closed the restaurant at its location between Madison and Fifth avenues in order to relocate it to a larger building. At the old address he opened the new restaurant, Café Boulud, named for the gathering place tended by his great-grandparents on their farm outside Lyons, France. The recipes he submitted for his last supper are all served at the newly opened Café Boulud.

Menu

Jerusalem artichoke soup with
sage garlic croutons

Braised spiced fresh pork belly with lentils

Oven-roasted vegetable casserole

Cod, cockles, and chorizo Basquaise

Jerusalem Artichoke Soup with
Sage Garlic Croutons

SOUP

4 tablespoons unsalted butter

3 ounces pancetta or smoked bacon, cut into 3 chunks

1 large Spanish onion, peeled and sliced

1 fennel bulb, cleaned and sliced

1 medium leek, white part only, cleaned and sliced

1 celery stalk, cleaned and sliced

3 garlic cloves, peeled and crushed

Bouquet garni: 2 sage sprigs, 2 thyme sprigs, 1 bay leaf

2 pounds Jerusalem artichokes, scrubbed and cut into ¼-inch slices, or 8 to 10 globe artichoke hearts

2 quarts unsalted chicken stock

½ tablespoon coarse salt

1 small potato, peeled and diced

Salt and freshly ground pepper, to taste

½ carton heavy cream

Melt the butter in a large dutch oven over medium heat. Add the pancetta and cook 3 to 5 minutes, stirring occasionally, until it renders its fat. Add the onion, fennel, leek, celery, garlic, and bouquet garni and cook, stirring from time to time. Add the artichokes and cook 15 to 20 minutes more. Pour in the stock, add the potato and coarse salt, and bring the mixture to a boil. Lower the heat so that the soup simmers and cook, uncovered, for 30 to 35 minutes, skimming the foam from the surface as needed. Spoon out the pieces of pancetta and cut them into small dice; set aside until serving time. Discard the bouquet garni.

Using an electric or immersion blender (a food processor will also work), puree the soup until it is very smooth. Strain through a fine-meshed sieve and taste for salt and pepper, adding seasoning as needed. Add the cream to the soup and reheat the soup over low heat while you make the croutons. The soup can be made ahead, chilled, and refrigerated overnight in a container with a tight-fitting lid. Reheat over gentle heat before serving.

CROUTONS

2 tablespoons unsalted butter

1 carton ⅓-inch diced country bread, crust removed

3 fresh sage leaves

1 garlic clove, peeled and crushed

Salt and freshly ground pepper

Warm the butter in a sauté pan over medium heat. Add the bread, sage, and garlic, season with salt and pepper, and sauté until the bread is crisp and golden brown. Discard the garlic and drain the croutons on a double thickness of paper towels.

Braised Spiced Fresh Pork Belly with Lentils

3 star anise

2 cinnamon sticks

½ teaspoon cloves

4 teaspoons black peppercorns

2 teaspoons coriander seeds

1 teaspoon fennel seeds

1 cup coarse salt

¼ cup sugar

1 teaspoon finely chopped, peeled garlic

4 pounds slab fresh, lean pork belly on the bone

1½ cups dark green lentils (lentils du Puy)

2 large carrots, 1 left whole, 1 cut into ½-inch dice

2 celery stalks, 1 left whole, 1 cut into ½-inch dice

1 large onion, peeled, half left whole, half cut into ½-inch dice

4 thyme sprigs

4 rosemary sprigs

4 sage leaves

3 bay leaves

1 small bunch of parsley, stems reserved and leaves chopped

1 tablespoon olive oil

1 pound baby back ribs

Salt and freshly ground pepper

1 cinnamon stick

1 teaspoon black peppercorns

¼ teaspoon fennel seeds

1 star anise

2 cloves

½ teaspoon coriander seeds

2 garlic cloves, peeled

2 tablespoons maple syrup

1 bottle chardonnay or other dry white wine (750 ml)

4 quarts chicken stock

TO CURE THE PORK BELLY

Preheat oven to 300 degrees. Combine star anise, cinnamon, cloves, black peppercorns, coriander, and fennel seeds on a sheet tray and toast in oven for 5 minutes. Using a mortar and pestle or a clean, heavy-bottomed pot, crush spices completely. Combine with the salt, sugar, and garlic. Using a sharp knife, score pork skin with a crisscross of 1-inch squares approximately ⅛-inch deep and place in a flat-bottomed container. Rub with spice, salt, and sugar mixture. Cover with plastic wrap and refrigerate for 48 hours.

TO COOK THE PORK AND LENTILS

Place lentils in a bowl and cover with cold water. Soak for 1 hour and drain before using. Scrape spice and salt mixture from pork and discard. Rinse pork briefly under running water to remove excess spices. Place pork in a pot along with whole carrot, celery, and onion half, pour in enough water to cover pork by 1 to 2 inches and bring to a boil. Tie together 2 thyme sprigs, 2 rosemary sprigs, 2 sage leaves, 2 bay leaves, and parsley stems and add to the pot. Simmer 40 minutes, regularly skimming off fat that rises to surface. Add lentils and simmer 20 minutes more. Remove from heat and transfer pork belly and whole vegetables to a plate. Discard herbs and drain lentils. Place lentils in a covered pan and set aside.

Preheat oven to 300 degrees. Heat olive oil in a casserole over high heat. Season baby back ribs with salt and pepper and add to pot. Brown evenly for 5 to 7 minutes. Add diced vegetables, remaining herbs (except parsley leaves), spices, and garlic and brown for 5 to 7 minutes more, stirring frequently. Add maple syrup and cook 1 to 2 minutes until caramelized. Add white wine and return pork belly to pot, resting it on ribs and vegetables. Place in oven and cook 30 minutes, basting every 10 to 15 minutes. Add chicken broth and cook for 2½ hours more, basting as before.

While pork is braising, cut reserved whole vegetables into ¼-inch dice and add to pot with lentils. When very tender remove pork belly and ribs from pot and set aside. Ribs can be cooled, refrigerated, and used in a salad. Degrease and then strain liquid, discarding vegetables and herbs, and reduce on top of stove until there are 3 cups left. Set 1 cup aside to serve as a sauce alongside the pork.

Add 1 cup to lentils along with chopped parsley and rewarm over medium heat 5 to 10 minutes while finishing the pork. Return final cup to casserole along with pork belly and reduce over high heat, basting pork constantly until liquid turns into a glaze and top of pork belly is well coated and shiny.

Place a mound of lentils in center of each warm serving plate. Place a square of fresh pork belly on top and drizzle sauce around lentils.

Oven-Roasted Vegetable Casserole

5 tablespoons olive oil, plus extra for serving

8 small turnips (8 ounces), peeled with a knife

8 small to medium fingerling potatoes, washed

8 medium cippoline onions (8 ounces), peeled

8 California carrots, peeled and shaped

8 medium white mushrooms, cleaned and stems removed

8 medium round pink radishes, washed and trimmed

8 3-inch-long pieces of celery stalk, peeled

2 large garlic cloves, peeled

Bouquet garni: 1 bay leaf, 1 thyme sprig, and reserved basil stems

1 teaspoon crushed coriander seeds

Salt and freshly ground pepper

½ cup niçoise olives

2 ounces basil, washed, leaves and stems separated

1 lemon, cut into 4 wedges

Fleur de sel (or other high-quality salt)

Grated Pecorino Romano or Parmesan cheese

Preheat oven to 350 degrees. Heat 3 tablespoons of olive oil in a large casserole over medium heat. When hot, add the turnips and potatoes and roast, tossing frequently, on top of the stove for 8 to 10 minutes until the vegetables brown lightly. Add the remaining olive oil, onions, carrots, mushrooms, radishes, celery, garlic, bouquet garni, and crushed coriander seeds. Season with salt and pepper and roast for an additional 8 to 10 minutes, tossing regularly to color the vegetables lightly and evenly as before.

Place the casserole in the oven and roast for approximately 30 minutes, stirring occasionally, or until all the vegetables are tender to a knife. Remove from the oven and discard the bouquet garni and garlic cloves. Add the olives and half of the basil leaves to the casserole and toss well. Place the remaining basil leaves on top of the vegetables and serve immediately.

Present the vegetables in the casserole and serve the lemon wedges, extra olive oil, and fleur de sel on the side. If desired, Pecorino Romano or Parmesan cheese may also be sprinkled on the vegetables when serving.

Cod, Cockles, and Chorizo Basquaise

FOR THE VEGETABLE PIPERADE AND CHORIZO

1 tablespoon olive oil

4 ounces chorizo, cut in half lengthwise
and then into ¼-inch slices

1 medium onion, peeled,
cut in half lengthwise and then into
¼-inch slices

1 red pepper, cut in half lengthwise,
seeded, and cut into ¼-inch slices

1 green pepper, cut in half lengthwise,
seeded, and cut into ¼-inch slices

4 plum tomatoes, peeled,
cut into 4 wedges, and seeded

2 garlic cloves, peeled, germ removed,
and finely diced

1 pinch of hot pepper flakes

Salt and freshly ground pepper

Heat the olive oil in a large sauté pan over medium heat. When hot, add the chorizo and brown evenly for 3 to 4 minutes. Using a slotted spoon, transfer the chorizo to a plate and set aside. Add the onion and peppers to the pan and sweat, without color, for approximately 10 to 12 minutes, or until the onion is translucent. Return the chorizo to the pan along with the tomato, garlic, and hot pepper flakes. Season with salt and pepper, mix well, and cover. Lower the heat and cook for another 10 to 12 minutes.

The piperade may be prepared in advance, cooled and stored in the refrigerator overnight. Rewarm gently while preparing the cod and cockles.

FOR THE COD AND COCKLES

4 tablespoons olive oil

4 cod fillets, 6 ounces each, skin on

Salt and freshly ground pepper

2 teaspoons flour

24 cockles or 12 littleneck clams, rinsed

1 thyme sprig

1 garlic clove, peeled

4 parsley sprigs, leaves only

¼ cup white wine

After covering the vegetables, heat 2 tablespoons of olive oil in wide-bottomed shallow pot over medium to high heat. Season the cod fillets with salt and pepper and dust the skin side lightly with flour. When the oil is hot, add the cod to the pan, skin side down, and brown for 4 minutes. Flip the cod fillets over; add the cockles, thyme, garlic, parsley leaves, and white wine around the cod and cover. Lower the heat to medium and steam for 5 minutes. Discard the thyme and garlic. Remove the cod and cockles from the pan and keep warm aside. Strain the *jus* into a blender and blend with 1 tablespoon of olive oil to emulsify.

Mound the vegetables and chorizo in the centers of 4 warm, shallow serving bowls. Place the cod on top and arrange 6 cockles per person around the fish. Spoon the *jus* over the cockles and drizzle the remaining tablespoon of olive oil over the cod fillets.

TOM DOUGLAS

Dahlia Lounge, Etta's, and Palace Kitchen: Seattle, Washington

"IF AN OUT-OF-TOWNER could spend only one night in Seattle, this is the place to eat," reported one reviewer of Tom Douglas's Dahlia Lounge restaurant. Another called the restaurant owner Seattle's "most brilliant, iconoclastic chef." The owner of two other eateries in Seattle—Etta's and Palace Kitchen—chef Douglas is considered one of the country's up-and-coming culinary innovators. It was a circuitous route that got him where he is today. A native of Delaware, Douglas began his career cooking at the Hotel DuPont in Wilmington but then struck out for Seattle in 1978, where he traded in his chef's apron for a box of carpenter's tools. He tried his hand at home building, railroad car repair, and, finally, wine selling before deciding that cooking was too much in his blood to ignore. In 1984 he took a chef's position at Seattle's Café Sport, where he honed his culinary skills. In 1989 he opened his first restaurant, the Dahlia Lounge, and proceeded to win wide acclaim for his culinary skills, including the James Beard Association Award for Best Northwest Chef. Today he is considered one of the originators of the modern Northwest style, or Pacific Rim Cuisine, as it sometimes is called, and his restaurants are among the most popular in the Northwest.

Menu

Tom's tasty tuna salad with green onion pancakes

Chinese BBQ'd duck with aromatic rice

Long beans in black bean sauce

Coconut cream pie

Tom's Tasty Tuna Salad with Green Onion Pancakes

1 pound cleaned and boned
  sushi-grade tuna, cut into
  ¼-inch cubes

⅓ cup chopped scallions

1 heaping cup fresh bean sprouts

⅓ cup loosely packed fresh cilantro

½ cup or more sake sauce (see recipe)

1½ tablespoons peanut oil

1 teaspoon Oriental sesame oil

Scallion pancakes (see recipe)

Lime wedges, for garnish

Radishes, for garnish

Fresh cucumber pickles

Place the tuna cubes in a bowl with the scallions, bean sprouts, and cilantro. Add enough sake sauce to coat everything well. Toss gently. Drizzle with the peanut and sesame oils and toss gently again. To serve, place equal amounts of tuna salad on each of four plates and garnish with one scallion pancake, lime wedges, radishes, and cucumber pickles.

SAKE SAUCE

½ cup sake (Japanese rice wine)

¼ cup soy sauce

¼ cup rice vinegar

¼ teaspoon chopped garlic

1 serrano chili pepper, seeded and
  chopped

½ teaspoon chopped fresh ginger

1 tablespoon sugar

The sauce must be chilled before dressing the tuna, so plan ahead. It can be stored, tightly sealed, in the refrigerator for up to one week.

Combine the sake, soy sauce, rice vinegar, garlic, chili pepper, ginger, and sugar in a small saucepan over medium-low heat and cook, stirring, until the sugar dissolves. Remove from the heat and allow to cool slightly at room temperature before refrigerating. Store, covered, in the refrigerator until well chilled. Makes approximately 1 cup.

GREEN ONION PANCAKES

2 teaspoons sesame seeds

1 large egg

2 teaspoons Oriental sesame oil

4 8-inch flour tortillas

2 scallions, finely chopped

2 tablespoons vegetable oil, or more as
needed

In a small skillet over medium heat, toast the sesame seeds until golden, shaking the pan often. It should take less than 5 minutes; watch that they don't burn. Transfer the seeds to a small bowl or plate and set aside. In a small bowl lightly beat the egg with the sesame oil. Brush one side of each tortilla with the egg mixture to coat lightly—you will not use all the egg wash. Sprinkle each tortilla with the scallions and sesame seeds. Fold the tortillas in half, pressing down to seal. Heat the vegetable oil in a 10-inch skillet over medium heat. Add 2 pancakes at a time and cook until lightly browned on both sides, about 2 minutes on each side, using more oil as needed. Transfer the pancakes to a plate and cover to keep warm until ready to serve. Serves 4.

Note: There are two kinds of sesame oil. Regular sesame oil is light in color, cold pressed, and well suited for stir-frying with its high burning point of 440 degrees. The darker Oriental sesame oil is more strongly flavored, so this nutty-tasting extract from sesame seeds is used in salad dressings and in meat and poultry marinades. Oriental sesame oil is available in Asian markets, health and specialty food stores, and some supermarkets. It goes wonderfully with such flavors as scallions, ginger, and garlic.

TODD ENGLISH

Olives and Figs of Charlestown, Massachusetts

TODD ENGLISH seemed to have a plan from the very beginning. At the age of 15, when his contemporaries were focusing on the nuances and vagaries of teenage exploration, English was learning the workings of a professional kitchen. By the age of 20, he had graduated with honors from The Culinary Institute of America and traveled to Italy, where he apprenticed at the well-established Dal Pescatore in Canto Sull O'lio and Paraccuchi in Locando D'Angello. When he returned to the United States at the age of 25, he opened the restaurant Michela's in Cambridge, Massachusetts, where he served as executive chef until he was able to open the restaurant Olives, with locations in Charlestown and Las Vegas, Nevada, and the restaurant Figs, which has locations in Charlestown, Boston, Wellesley, and Chestnutt Hill, Massachusetts. English has been featured in almost every food-related magazine and has won every award imaginable. He has written two cookbooks, *The Olives Table* and *The Figs Table*.

Menu

Foie Gras Flan

Toro (raw tuna)

Five Clam Chowder

White Truffles and Spaghetti

Chocolate Hash Browns

1959 Petrus wine

Todd English's Five Clam Chowder

CHOWDER BROTH

¼ cup butter

3 corn cobs (corn kernels removed)

2 leeks, diced

½ head of garlic

¾ onion, chopped

¼ bunch thyme

Bacon rind or smoked ham hock

1 stalk celery chopped

4 quahog clams

Salt and pepper, to taste

¼ cup white wine

3 cups chicken broth, fresh or canned

Melt butter in a 4-quart pot and add corn cobs, leeks, garlic, onion, thyme, bacon rind, celery, quahogs, salt, and pepper. Cook until the onions are translucent—no color on vegetable. Add white wine and chicken broth and simmer until the quahogs are open. Strain and reserve broth.

BLISSFUL MASHED POTATOES

8 medium red bliss potatoes

¼ cup butter

½ cup heavy cream

Salt and pepper

Cook potatoes in salted water until soft. Heat the butter and heavy cream. Strain the potatoes and add warm cream and butter. Mash potatoes and season to taste.

3 tablespoon butter

¾ cup shucked corn

1 cup creamy corn

3 tablespoon minced garlic

1 tablespoon chopped thyme

12 cockles

12 littleneck clams

12 steamer clams

12 mahoganies

6 razor clams

¼ cup chicken broth

½ cup heavy cream

1 stalk celery, diced

Salt and pepper

¼ cup diced, rendered bacon

STEAMING CLAMS

In a 16" hotel pan, melt butter and add corn, garlic, and chopped thyme. Next add all clams and chicken broth. Cover and steam until clams are open.

TO ASSEMBLE

Warm the reserve broth, add cream, diced celery, salt, pepper, and rendered bacon. Warm blissful mash. Place a dollop of blissful mashed potatoes in each bowl. Pile 2 cockles, 2 mahoganies, 1 razor, 2 littlenecks, and 2 steamers on top. Ladle 8 ounces of chowder broth over clams and adjust the seasoning. Serve.

MARIO FERRARI

Mario's: Nashville, Tennessee

MARIO'S IS ONE of the best-kept secrets in Nashville, except among the stars of country music and a host of peripatetic restaurant critics who have heaped accolades upon the restaurant for more than 30 years. Every year for the past six years, *The Wine Spectator* has awarded the restaurant its "Best of Award of Excellence." It has been chosen one of the top 10 Italian restaurants in America by *Veronelli* and received similar honors from the *Mobil Travel Guide* and the *Robb Report*. Owner and chef Mario Ferarri built the restaurant's reputation on a menu of Northern Italian cuisine that puts special emphasis on veal, fish, and chicken, an ornate decor that contains antiques and oil paintings, and a wine list that boasts 721 selections. Ferrari designed his restaurant, which has three private dining rooms, with romance in mind, and it has served as a launching pad for countless trysts among country music's elite. As a matter of fact, visitors to Nashville intent on encountering romance-bound country music stars in the flesh are more likely to do so at the dimly lit Mario's than at any of the neon-wrapped honky-tonk palaces that populate the city. For his last supper Ferrari chose a dish prepared by former Mario's chef Giovanni Giosa.

Chef Giovanni's Goat Cheese Soufflé

6 tablespoons unsalted butter, melted

5 tablespoons flour

1½ cups half-and-half

1 cup heavy cream

Salt, pepper, nutmeg, and cayenne, to taste

5 egg yolks, beaten

6 ounces Montrachet cheese, shredded

1 cup egg whites, stiffly beaten

Thyme

Blend butter and flour in saucepan. Cook until bubbly, stirring constantly. Stir in half-and-half and cream gradually. Cook until thickened, stirring constantly. Season with salt, pepper, nutmeg, and cayenne pepper. Remove from heat. Add a small amount of hot mixture to egg yolks to temper the yolks; then gradually stir egg yolks back into hot cream mixture. Cook until very thick, stirring constantly.

Add two-thirds of the cheese. Stir until melted. Fold one-third of the egg whites gently into cheese mixture. Fold in remaining egg whites gently. Spoon into soufflé dish. Sprinkle with remaining cheese and thyme. Bake in a preheated 325-degree oven for 50 to 60 minutes or until puffed, brown, and set.

ROLAND PASSOT

La Folie: San Francisco, California

ROLAND PASSOT started his culinary career at the age of 15 in Lyons, France, where he worked with many fine chefs while he was going to school. He began his American career in Chicago with chef Jean Banchet at Le Français, and then made a name for himself at the Adolphus French Room in Dallas and Le Castel in San Francisco. By 1988 Passot, his wife, Jamie, and his brother opened La Folie restaurant in San Francisco. Two years later the James Beard Foundation honored him with the title of "Rising Star Chef in America." Over the past decade Passot has made La Folie one of the most-heralded French restaurants in the country. What makes him distinctive is his decision to forgo the rich, traditional sauces associated with French cuisine in favor of lighter sauces constructed of vegetable juices and lesser amounts of salt and sugar.

Menu

"Tzar Nicoulai" golden osetra caviar on potato
blinis with salmon, asparagus,
and crème fraîche

Napoleon of seared Cape Cod sea scallops with
Yukon gold potatoes, winter truffles,
and an asparagus emulsion

Parsley and garlic soup with a ragout of snails
and shiitake mushrooms

Lobster fricassee in a roasted pumpkin with a
ragout of seasonal vegetables/sauce homardine

Roasted quail and foie gras with a simple salad
and wild mushrooms, natural juice
with roasted garlic

Roasted Canadian venison with a potato, leek,
prune "gateau," sauce poivrade with
Scharfeenberger chocolat essence

Wild blackberry tea crème brûlée with
orange lace tuiles

Guest List

Jules Verne,
a dreamer of the future

Nostradamus,
a visionary of the future

Fernand Point,
the father of nouvelle cuisine

Lumière brothers,
creators of cinematography

Jean-Luc Picard,
who as a fictional personage was always traveling
where no one has gone before,
discovering new worlds with no limit in the universe

Brillat-Savarin,
Le Prince des Gastronomes

My wife, Jamie, who has a great
imagination; and my children,
Charlotte and Jean Paul.
I would not want them to miss that dinner.

Wild Blackberry Tea Crème Brûlée

8 cups heavy cream

Blackberry tea

16 egg yolks

2 cups sugar

Pinch of salt

Bring cream to a boil. Infuse blackberry tea to desired strength—usually the normal strength you prefer for your drinking tea. Whip the yolks and the sugar to a ribbon. Add salt. Temper cream into the egg mixture and mix well. Let rest and skim the foam. Fill up cups. Place cups in a bain-marie and cook in a preheated 275-degree oven for 1¼ hours. Serve cold. Yields 16 servings.

NORA POUILLON

Nora and Asia Nora: Washington, D.C.

ITNESS MAGAZINE recently honored Nora Pouillon as one of America's healthiest chefs. It was a double-edged honor, for not only is the chef and restaurant owner known for her healthful cuisine, but she is an outspoken advocate of physical fitness and often can be spotted walking on a path between Restaurant Nora's location in Washington's Dupont Circle and Asia Nora's downtown M Street location. An avid sportswoman, she likes to ski, rollerblade, swim, and hike. *The Washington Post* has called her one of the city's "power chefs," a description that is apt because of her seemingly tireless devotion to causes such as improving the quality of public-school cafeteria fare and advancing opportunities for women in the culinary profession. She is an active member of the Washington chapter of Les Dames d'Escoffier and the International Association of Women Chefs and Restaurateurs. Somehow, despite her busy schedule and varied interests, she has managed to write a cookbook, *Cooking with Nora*, a finalist for the 1996 Julia Child Cookbook Award.

Guest List

I would have my family, my four children. Then I would have someone like an Indian medicine man, a shaman, so we could talk about where I am going. I'd also like to have someone to entertain, a storyteller, someone who has interesting things to tell. It should be a fun party. Then I thought it would be nice to have a Renaissance man, like Leonardo da Vinci, someone artistic, and then a food person. It could be my idol Elizabeth David or James Beard or Emmitt Fisher. I would prefer to have my last supper in the winter in a mountain chalet. I am Austrian by birth, so mountains would make me feel more calm and comfortable.

Menu

Champagne and caviar

Clear wild mushroom soup

Butternut squash puree

Potato gratin

Spit roast

Belgian endive, mâche, beets & apple with walnuts & sherry vinaigrette

Chocolate almond cake with chocolate glaze

Clear Wild Mushroom Soup

1½ tablespoons olive oil

2 tablespoons minced shallots

1 teaspoon minced garlic

1 small leek, white part only,
   thinly sliced

1 small carrot, peeled and chopped

2 ribs celery, chopped

¾ pound assorted wild mushrooms:
   chanterelle, hen of the woods,
   porcini, shiitake, cremini,
   or portobello

1 tablespoon tamari

3 cups chicken or vegetable stock or
   water with 2 chicken bouillon cubes

Sea salt and freshly ground pepper

1½ tablespoons chopped flat leaf
   parsley or tarragon, for garnish

Heat the olive oil in a medium saucepan, add the shallots and garlic, and sauté on a medium flame, stirring often until soft, about 4 to 5 minutes. Stir in the leek, carrot, celery, and wild mushrooms and sauté until the mixture is softened, about 4 to 5 minutes. Add the tamari, the chicken or vegetable stock, or water with bouillon cubes and bring to a boil. Reduce the heat, cover, and simmer for about 20 minutes. Season to taste with salt and pepper.

Assembly: Ladle the wild mushroom soup into one of four warm soup bowls and sprinkle with chopped parsley or tarragon.

Butternut Squash Puree

2 butternut squashes,
   about 1½ pounds, peeled, seeded,
   and cut into 1-inch cubes

Pinch of mace or allspice

Sea salt and freshly ground black
   pepper

Steam the squash for about 20 minutes or until tender, using a collapsible steamer insert in a saucepan. Puree the squash in a food processor. Season to taste with the mace or allspice and salt and pepper. If the puree is too thick, add some water.

Potato Gratin

1 pound peeled potatoes,
  sliced very thinly

Butter

1 clove garlic

Salt and freshly ground black pepper

10 fluid ounces cream

Preheat oven to 310 degrees. Rinse the potato slices in cold water and pat dry using a clean cloth. Butter a shallow, preferably earthenware gratin dish and rub with garlic clove. Layer the potato slices, seasoning with salt and pepper as you go. Pour cream over, dot with small pieces of butter and cook for 1 to 1½ hours. Turn the oven up fairly high for the last 10 minutes to allow the potatoes to crisp and turn a golden brown on top.

Belgian Endive, Mâche, Beets & Apple with Walnut & Sherry Vinaigrette

8 small beets (about ½ pound)

¼ cup English walnut halves

4 heads Belgian endive

1 apple, cored, thinly sliced

Preheat oven to 350 degrees.

Steam the beets for 12 to 15 minutes in a small, covered saucepan, using a collapsible steamer. Allow to cool. Arrange the walnuts on a baking sheet and bake them in the oven for 8 to 10 minutes or until fragrant and toasted. Peel and quarter the cooked beets. Wipe the outside of the Belgian endive with a damp cloth, trim the base and separate the leaves.

SHERRY VINAIGRETTE

Mix the salt, pepper, and sherry vinegar in a small bowl until the salt dissolves. Add the olive oil slowly, whisking with a fork.

ASSEMBLY

Sea salt and freshly ground
  black pepper

1 tablespoon sherry vinegar

3 tablespoons extra-virgin olive oil

4 to 6 ounces mâche or watercress,
  washed and spun dry

4 ounces Brie

Just before serving, toss the mâche or watercress with some of the sherry vinaigrette. Divide the greens among the four dinner-size plates, placing them in the center of each plate. Arrange the Belgian endive and the apple slices around the edge of the greens. Add beets and slices of Brie to each salad and sprinkle with the walnuts. Drizzle the remaining sherry vinaigrette over the endive leaves.

Chocolate Almond Cake with Chocolate Glaze

1½ cups almonds

4 ounces unsalted butter

Flour, for dusting

¾ cup bread crumbs

4 ounces semisweet chocolate

¾ cup sugar

6 egg yolks

6 egg whites

Preheat oven to 325 degrees. Arrange the almonds on a baking sheet and bake them in the oven for 8 to 10 minutes or until they are fragrant and toasted. You don't need to stir them during baking. Let the nuts cool. Grind the almonds in a minichopper or food processor until fine. Butter an 8-inch springform pan with about a teaspoon of butter and dust with flour or some of the bread crumbs. Melt the chocolate in a double boiler over simmering water. Remove from the heat and allow to cool. Combine the butter, sugar, and cool, melted chocolate in the bowl of a mixer and beat until the batter changes to a lighter color and becomes creamy, about 5 minutes. Scrape down the sides of the bowl once or twice while beating. Add egg yolks, one at a time, continuing to beat. Lower the speed of the mixer and add the ground almonds and bread crumbs. Beat the egg whites until they are soft but not stiff. Fold a third of the beaten whites into the batter, blending it thoroughly. Gently fold in the remaining whites, working quickly and carefully to incorporate all the whites without deflating the batter. Pour the batter into the prepared pan and smooth the top. Bake for 50 to 55 minutes in a preheated 325 degree oven or until a toothpick inserted in the center comes out clean. Allow the cake to cool in the pan for 10 minutes before turning it out onto a cake rack. Let the cake cool completely before adding the glaze.

CHOCOLATE GLAZE

3 ounces semisweet chocolate

3 ounces unsalted butter, softened

1 ounce milk chocolate at room temperature for garnish

Melt the chocolate in a double boiler over simmering water. Add the butter and stir until blended and smooth. Remove the glaze from the heat and allow to cool and thicken to the consistency of thick cream. Brush the cake to remove any loose crumbs and place both the cake and the cooling rack on a sheet pan to catch the chocolate glaze. Slowly pour a pool of chocolate glaze at the center of the cake. Working from the center out, use a long, metal spatula to spread the glaze evenly over the top and sides of the cake. For a smoother look, glaze the cake a second time (optional). Scoop up the excess glaze from the sheet pan and reheat it in a small double boiler. Pour it through a sieve, if necessary, to remove any cake crumbs and cool it slightly to thicken a bit. Pour the glaze again at the center of the top and allow it to spread without using a spatula. With a vegetable peeler shave off some curls of the milk chocolate and sprinkle them on top of the cake. Allow the glaze to set for about 2 hours at room temperature or 20 minutes in the refrigerator. Serve with light whipped cream.

STEPHAN PYLES

Star Canyon and AquaKnox: Dallas, Texas

STEPHAN PYLES has been called one of the founding fathers of modern Southwestern cuisine. *Bon Appétit* magazine credits him with "almost single-handedly" changing the cooking scene in Texas. In *The New York Times*, Craig Claiborne wrote that the Dallas-based chef and restaurant owner had raised Southwestern cuisine "to the level of art ... he is an absolute genius in the kitchen." *Gourmet* magazine says that "if you only eat one meal in Dallas," eat it at Pyles's Star Canyon restaurant.

Since Star Canyon opened in 1994, it consistently has been listed among the best restaurants in America. Pyles's newest restaurant, AquaKnox, also has received rave reviews since its opening in 1997. Of course, Pyles's acclaim in the 1990s as an innovative chef did not happen overnight. Throughout the 1980s, while chef and owner of two restaurants, Routh Street Café and Baby Routh, he racked up a string of awards, including the James Beard Foundation's award for Best Chef in America-Southwest, *Nation's Restaurant News'* Fine Dining Hall of Fame Award, and Restaurants and Institutions' Ivy Award.

Pyles has cooked for Queen Elizabeth II and Mikhail Gorbachev, and he was one of five chefs invited to prepare dinner for Jimmy Carter's 70th birthday. He is the author of two cookbooks, *Tamales* and *The New Texas Cuisine*, which includes the recipes he chose for his last supper. His nationally syndicated television series, *New Tastes from Texas*, is aired on PBS.

Menu

Chilled shrimp and jicama soup with
fresh goat's buttermilk and basil

Honey fried chicken
with thyme-mint cream sauce

Spicy whipped sweet potatoes and
gumbo z'herbs

Peanut butter–banana cream pie
with hot fudge

Chilled Shrimp and Jicama Soup
Fresh Goat's Buttermilk and Basil

1 medium (about 8 ounces) cucumber, peeled, seeded, and chopped

¼ cup raspberry vinegar

1½ pounds jicama, peeled and cut into ¼-inch dice (about 5 cups)

1 tablespoon plus 2 teaspoons sugar

2 teaspoons salt, plus extra

8 ounces small raw shrimp, peeled and deveined

½ teaspoon cayenne powder

2 tablespoons olive oil

2 cups goat's buttermilk or cultured buttermilk

1 cup heavy cream

1 cup sour cream

½ cup packed chopped basil leaves

1 yellow bell pepper, roasted, peeled and cut into ¼" x 1" strips

1 medium red bell pepper, roasted, peeled and cut into ¼" x 1" strips

In a food processor puree the cucumber with the raspberry vinegar for about 30 seconds, until smooth. In a large bowl toss the jicama and cucumber puree together. Mix in the sugar and 1 teaspoon salt. Let the mixture stand while preparing the shrimp.

Place the shrimp in a medium bowl and sprinkle with the remaining teaspoon of salt and the cayenne. In a large skillet over high heat, heat the olive oil until lightly smoking. Add the shrimp and cook until they turn pink, about 2 minutes. Remove the shrimp and set aside.

In a large bowl combine the buttermilk and heavy cream; then whisk in the sour cream. Add the jicama-vinegar mix, the reserved shrimp, the basil, and the roasted bell peppers, and combine. Season with salt to taste and serve.

My source for goat's buttermilk is Paula Lambert's Mozzarella Company in Dallas, but the buttermilk can be made like crème fraîche by adding cultured buttermilk to goat's milk and allowing it to sit at room temperature overnight. Goat's milk is usually available at health food stores, but you can substitute regular buttermilk if necessary.

Honey-Fried Chicken
with Thyme-Mint Cream Sauce

1 chicken, about 3 pounds

½ cup honey

2 tablespoons raspberry or other fruit vinegar

½ cup flour

2 tablespoons whole-wheat flour

2 teaspoons cayenne powder

2 eggs

¼ cup buttermilk

1 cup vegetable oil

Salt and freshly ground pepper, to taste

Cut the chicken into serving pieces (preferably 6) and place in a mixing bowl, reserving the backbone, neck, and wings for the stock. Stir the honey and vinegar together and pour over the chicken. Let marinate for at least 2 hours, mixing occasionally.

In a separate mixing bowl, combine the flours and cayenne and set aside. In another mixing bowl, whisk the eggs and buttermilk. Preheat the oven to 200 degrees.

In a large skillet, heat the oil over medium-high heat to 300 degrees (cooking at a low temperature will prevent the honey from caramelizing too quickly and burning). Remove the chicken from the marinade and drain on paper towels. Dip the chicken in the egg wash, season with salt and pepper, and dredge in the flour-cayenne mixture, coating thoroughly. Strain the marinade and reserve 1 tablespoon for the sauce.

Starting with the dark meat first, gently drop the chicken pieces into the hot oil for 5 to 6 minutes on the first side until browned. Turn the pieces, add the white meat, and continue cooking, adjusting the heat so that the chicken browns evenly on both sides without burning. Turn once more and cook until well browned and tender when pierced with a fork. The dark meat should cook for 15 to 18 minutes and the white meat 10 to 12 minutes. Transfer the chicken to the oven and keep warm while making the sauce.

THYME-MINT CREAM SAUCE

½ cup dry white wine

½ cup chicken stock

1½ cups heavy cream

1½ tablespoons chopped mint

1 tablespoon chopped thyme

1 teaspoon lemon zest

1 tablespoon reserved marinade

Salt and freshly ground pepper,
   to taste

To prepare the sauce, pour the oil from the skillet, leaving any bits on the bottom. Deglaze the pan with the white wine and add the chicken stock. Reduce the liquid by half over medium-high heat, 3 to 4 minutes. Add the cream, mint, thyme, lemon zest, and reserved marinade and reduce until the sauce is thick enough to coat the back of a spoon, 5 to 6 minutes. Strain the sauce and season with salt and pepper.

Spicy Whipped Sweet Potatoes

2 large sweet potatoes, peeled
   and diced

½ white potato, peeled and diced

6 tablespoons pure maple syrup

1 teaspoon cayenne powder

1 tablespoon pure chili powder

2 teaspoons salt

8 tablespoons unsalted butter (1 stick),
   room temperature

In a saucepan, bring the potatoes to a boil, reduce the heat and simmer for 15 minutes, until soft. Drain and transfer the potatoes to a food processor. Add the maple syrup, cayenne, chili powder, and salt. Process for 1 minute while adding the butter 1 tablespoon at a time. Warm in a pan and serve.

Gumbo Z'herbs

1 bunch radish greens

1 bunch turnip greens

1 bunch watercress

1 bunch carrot tops

6 scallions, chopped

5 cups chicken stock

1 tablespoon unsalted butter

8 ounces cooked sausage, such as lasso or andouille, diced

1 small white onion, chopped

2 cloves garlic, minced

1 tablespoon chopped basil or parsley

1 teaspoon chopped thyme

Salt and freshly ground black pepper to taste

1 bay leaf

1 teaspoon filé gumbo

Cayenne powder, to taste

Wash all the greens thoroughly. Place in a large saucepan with the scallions and stock, and simmer for 10 minutes. Strain the greens and reserve the stock. Finely chop the greens and set aside.

Heat the butter in a large skillet and sauté the sausage over medium-high heat for about 10 minutes. Add the onion, garlic, and basil or parsley, and sauté until the onion and garlic turn golden brown. Add the greens and simmer for 15 minutes. Transfer to a large pan with the reserved stock and add the greens and all the remaining seasonings. Cover and simmer for 20 minutes.

Peanut Butter–Banana Cream Pie

¼ cup banana liqueur

½ teaspoon unflavored powdered
   gelatin

2¾ cups milk

½ vanilla bean, halved lengthwise and
   scraped

4 eggs, separated (whites reserved
   at room temperature)

1½ cups sugar

5 tablespoons cornstarch

2 ripe bananas

Juice of ½ lemon

¼ cup smooth peanut butter,
   at room temperature

1 9" baked pie crust

¾ cup chopped roasted peanuts

Pinch of salt

Pinch of cream of tartar

Place the banana liqueur in a small mixing bowl, sprinkle the gelatin on top, and allow to soften for 5 minutes. Place the bowl over simmering water until the gelatin is completely clear. Set aside.

In a saucepan combine the milk and vanilla bean. Bring to a boil, remove from the heat, cover, and allow to steep while preparing the yolk mixture.

In a mixing bowl whisk the egg yolks while gradually adding ¾ cup of sugar. When the yolks have lightened, whisk in the cornstarch. Strain the milk and gradually pour into the yolk mixture while stirring. Return to a clean saucepan set over medium heat and stir constantly until the mixture begins to boil. Reduce the heat and continue to stir for 2 to 3 minutes. Remove from the heat, whisk in the gelatin mixture, and incorporate thoroughly. Allow the pastry cream to cool completely.

Slice the bananas on the bias and brush with lemon juice. Whip the peanut butter to make it easier to spread; then spread on the top side of the pie crust. Sprinkle half of the peanuts on top of the peanut butter. Arrange half of the banana slices on top of the peanuts and spread the pastry cream over the bananas. Arrange the remaining banana slices over the pastry cream, and then sprinkle the remaining peanuts on top of the bananas. Refrigerate while making the meringue.

Preheat the oven to 400 degrees. Place the egg whites in a mixing bowl with the salt and cream of tartar. Beat with an electric mixer until soft peaks form. Gradually add the remaining ¾ cup of sugar while beating, until stiff peaks form and the meringue becomes glossy. Spread the meringue on top of the pie or place in a pastry bag and pipe on decoratively. Make sure the meringue touches the pie shell all over.

Place the pie in the oven for no more than 1 minute. Watch constantly and remove when the meringue is lightly browned. Refrigerate for at least 30 minutes before cutting.

BAKED PIE CRUST

1½ cups flour

¼ teaspoon salt

½ cup vegetable shortening

4 to 5 tablespoons cold water

Rice or dried beans, for weighting

1 egg white

In a mixing bowl, combine the flour and salt. Add the shortening and incorporate with your fingertips until the mixture resembles very coarse cornmeal. Sprinkle 3 to 4 tablespoons of the water over the flour mixture in tablespoon increments while stirring with a fork. Form the dough into a ball and let rest in the refrigerator for 1 hour.

On a lightly floured surface, roll out the dough into a circle to ⅛-inch thickness. Place the dough in a pie pan. Trim and crimp the edges. Place the shell in the freezer for 20 minutes. Preheat the oven to 425 degrees.

Remove the shell and prick the bottom and sides with a fork. Press foil snugly over the bottom and sides of the crust. Pour rice or dried beans over the foil and bake in the oven for about 6 minutes. Whisk together the egg white and remaining tablespoon of water in a bowl. Remove the foil from the pan and brush the sides and bottom of the crust with the egg wash. Return to the oven and bake for an additional 8 to 10 minutes. Let cool before adding the pie filling.

HOT FUDGE SAUCE

⅓ cup light corn syrup

¼ cup water

¾ cup sugar

¼ cup unsweetened cocoa powder

1 tablespoon chopped unsweetened chocolate

2 tablespoons unsalted butter

⅓ cup heavy cream

Boil the corn syrup for 1 minute in a small saucepan. Stir in the water. Use caution as the mixture may spatter.

Sift the sugar and cocoa together in a mixing bowl. Stir in the corn syrup mixture. Bring to a boil, stirring until the sugar is dissolved. Add the chocolate and butter and whisk until melted. Add the cream and return to a boil. Remove from the heat. The sauce can be prepared a day ahead of time. Reheat gently.

NORMAN VAN AKEN

Norman's: Coral Gables, Florida

CHEF NORMAN VAN AKEN is the owner of Norman's restaurant in Miami's historic Coral Gables district. Considered by many to be the father of New World Cuisine, he is the author of three books, including *Norman's New World Cuisine*, one of three cookbooks nominated in 1997 for the prestigious Julia Child/IACP Awards. In a review of that book, the *Miami Herald* wrote that "exuberance abounds" at Van Aken's "cutting edge" restaurant where he takes the "Hispanic and Caribbean influences he loves and fuses them into fabulous and beautifully presented New World dishes." In 1998 *Playboy* selected his restaurant as one of the top 25 in America, and the previous year *Condé Nast Traveler* included it in its "Top 10 Restaurants in America." Van Aken is the celebrity consulting chef for all United Airlines flights to and from all of the airline's Latin American and Caribbean destinations.

Menu

THE AMUSÉES
Charlie Trotter's caviar surprise
Thomas Keller's smoked salmon cone

COLD SHELLFISH
Douglas Rodriguez's trio of ceviches
Rob Boone's wild kanpachi with
big eye tuna tartare
Mitsuba, mango, and fresh wasabi foam

HOT APPETIZER
Emeril Lagasse's rabbit and andouille gumbo
Dean Fearing's quail and black bean tacos

Salad Course

Alice Water's Chino Ranch farm's
vegetable salad

Nicole Routhier's Vietnamese soft spring rolls

Foie Gras Course

Stephan Pyles's foie gras tamale

Todd English's foie gras ravioli

Fish Entrées

Nobu Matsuhisa's black cod with miso

Wolfgang Puck's sizzling catfish Chinois

Meat Entrées

Lulu Peyraud's fireplace spit-roasted leg of
lamb with rosemary and natural juices

Daniel Boulud's roasted pork belly with foie
gras stuffed roasted turnip, truffled pigs feet,
garlic, spinach (and truffles), and lentils

Cheeses

Alain Ducasses's cheese cart and artisanal
breads

Dessert Courses

Ruth Van Aken's lemon meringue pie

Janet Van Aken's German chocolate cake

Double espressos with Maida Heatter's biscotti
and Francois Payard's chocolates

Sommeliers by Proal Perry and Jeffrey Wolfe

Flowers by Georgia O'Keefe

Guest List

Nana, Grampy, Gra, Grandpa, Irv,
my father, Mark Twain, Albert Einstein,
Jimi Hendrix, M.F.K. Fisher, Dorothy Parker,
Charles Dickens, Billie Holiday, Jack Kerouac,
W. B. Yeats, T. S. Eliot, Dylan Thomas,
Pablo Picasso, William Shakespeare,
Louis Armstrong, Charlie Parker, Carl Jung,
Charles Bukowski, Thomas Jefferson,
McKinley Morganfield aka Muddy Waters,
Maya Angelou, and all of the (metaphorical
or otherwise) Red-Haired Girls

Note: I did not invite Jesus, Buddha, Lao-tzu,
or Elvis in that their presence might leave the
other guests speechless. The guests would rotate
seats after each course so that they would have
a chance to visit with each other as much as
possible. At a post-dinner party they would
dance off the food, talk, drink, and solve the
problems of the world.

Music

Stevie Ray Vaughan, Santana, Mozart,
John Lee Hooker, and a solo dramatic or
musical performance by Justin Van Aken

Note: I reserve the right to change this menu
and/or add or detract any guests based upon
the capriciousness of my moods, the tug of
imperfect remembrances, or the unfortunate
demise of anyone who would have made the list
had they not yet succumbed to mortality
between the time of the request of this list and
the actual publication of this book.

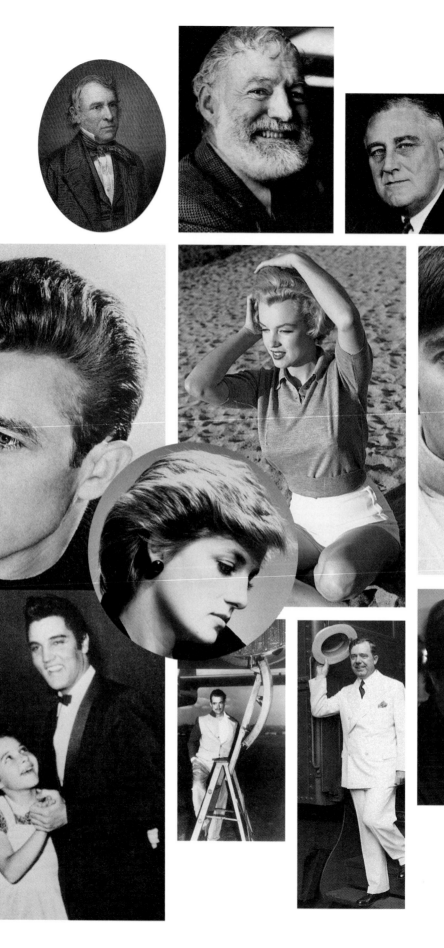

DECEASED CELEBRITIES

IT IS IMPOSSIBLE to read the wished-for last suppers of the celebrities who contributed to this book without wondering about the actual last suppers of those who have died and passed on (hopefully) to new adventures. I never had an opportunity to ask them what they would have wanted for their last suppers, but I did find ways to discover what they actually ate in the final hours of their lives.

Each last supper required its own special brand of investigative reporting. It meant poring over biographies and news articles to find references to last meals, and it meant digging up the names of the restaurants where they were last seen in public. Once the name of the restaurant was known, it required old-fashioned legwork to track down the waitresses or managers on duty that night. In the case of Ernest Hemingway, it took only one telephone call to discover that the restaurant where he enjoyed his last supper in Ketchum, Idaho, was still in business. But since the restaurant had changed hands several times in the intervening years, it required several additional telephone calls to locate the former owners—and more calls yet to locate the waitress who served him his last meal.

John Lennon offered a similar challenge. Once it was known that Lennon's last documented meal was at New York's Stage Deli, the challenge was in convincing the restaurant's managers and owners that it would not be a dishonor to the entertainer's memory or an invasion of his privacy to discuss his dining habits. Legwork, as applied to investigative reporting, is a misnomer, for it is talking that is the real exercise at work.

What is amazing, if you think about it, is that it is possible, after 10, 20, or 40 years, to go back in time to talk with a waitress or restaurant owner about what was on a celebrity's plate. That's really food for thought.

JOHN CANDY

Actor

1950–1994

CANADIAN-BORN JOHN CANDY got his start in show business in Toronto in 1974 with the formation of a spin-off of Chicago's Second City Comedy Troupe, but it did not take long for the heavyset actor to win the hearts of American audiences. He is probably best known for his comedic roles opposite *Saturday Night Live* alumni Dan Aykroyd, Steve Martin, and Bill Murray in such films as *The Blues Brothers, Stripes,* and *Planes, Trains and Automobiles,* but there were other sides to the actor that did not attract as much attention. He was a member of the musical group Northern Lights, which sang "Tears Are Not Enough" for the *We Are the World* album, and he was the co-owner of the Toronto Argonauts, one of the premier teams in the Canadian Football League. In 1994 he was on location in Mexico to film *Wagons East.* On the evening of March 3, 1994, the 300-pound actor cooked a late pasta dinner for himself and his assistants and then went to bed. He died in his sleep.

Last Supper

Pasta

JAMES DEAN

Actor

1931–1955

JAMES DEAN made only three films—*Rebel Without a Cause*, *East of Eden*, and *Giant*—but the actor achieved cult status during his brief, two-year career. Dean had a zest for life that encouraged comparisons with the doomed character he portrayed in *Rebel Without a Cause*. But even those who said he lived life too fast for his own good were stunned with the news of his violent death on September 30, 1955. The end came suddenly, without warning. Dean and a companion, Rolf Weutherich, were driving his racing Porsche north to Salinas, California, to compete in a race. At midafternoon they pulled off the highway to eat lunch at a restaurant named Tip's Diner. Dean's Porsche had less than 500 miles on it, and he was eager to see what it could do in a high-speed race. Perhaps because he was excited about the race, he had only a glass of milk for lunch. Later that afternoon, they stopped briefly at a small town, where Dean bought a bag of apples. Forty-five minutes later, Dean and Weutherich were speeding along Highway 466 toward an intersection when they spotted a Ford sedan going in the opposite direction. The sedan was driven by a 23-year-old college student, Donald Turnupseed. When Dean saw the sedan turning into the path of the Porsche, he told Weutherich: "That guy up there's gotta stop. He'll see us." Seconds later James Dean was dead, his head practically severed by the impact of the crash.

Last Supper

Glass of milk

Fresh apples

DIANA, PRINCESS OF WALES

Mother of Future King of England

1961–1997

THE ARRIVAL OF PRINCESS DIANA and Dodi Fayed at the Ritz Hotel in Paris is imprinted in our memory by virtue of the incessant television broadcasts of the event in the weeks and months following their tragic deaths in an automobile accident. That image has been shown and reshown until each of us has had the opportunity to memorize Diana's averted eyes and determined gait as she hurried into the hotel and retreated to the privacy of L'Espadon, the hotel's opulent dining room. Once there, Diana and Dodi found themselves in an area surrounded by mirrors. They ordered dinner, Dodi choosing grilled turbot and a bottle of Tattinger Champagne and Diana selecting the meal shown below. Unfortunately, by the time the meal arrived Diana had become unnerved by the mirrors and by a couple seated at a nearby table. The couple had a big paper bag at their feet, one that could contain a video camera, and they were looking at Diana and whispering. Diana told Dodi that she was uncomfortable in the dining room, so he suggested they leave and have their dinner sent to the Imperial Suite, where they could dine in private. It was the last dining experience either would ever have.

Last Supper

Asparagus and mushroom omelet

Dover sole with vegetable tempura

Champagne

ERNEST HEMINGWAY

Nobel Prize—winning Author

1899–1961

In 1961 Ernest Hemingway was one of the most revered and imitated writers in the world. Although his first novels were published in the 1920's, he continued to write with power and creativity into the 1950s. In 1953 he won a Pulitzer Prize for the book many critics consider his masterpiece, *The Old Man and the Sea*, and the following year his life's work was recognized with the Nobel Prize for Literature. The 1960s were a different matter. Personal problems and a changing literary environment left Hemingway despondent. In the spring of 1960, while he was being treated at the Mayo Clinic in Rochester, Minnesota, his wife, Mary, met with psychiatrists in an effort to have him hospitalized, but the move was thwarted by his physicians. On June 26 Mary and a friend, George Brown, drove him to their home in Ketchum, Idaho, arriving on June 30. The following day, they went to dinner at their favorite restaurant, the Christiania. Their waitress that evening was June Mallea, a 20-year-old native Idahoan who usually served the famous writer when he dined at the restaurant.

Thirty-eight years later, Mallea said she was not absolutely certain of everything Hemingway ordered that night, but she felt reasonably certain he had ordered the same thing he always ordered—a New York strip steak, which was accompanied by a baked potato and a green salad. Hemingway always substituted a Caesar salad for the traditional green salad. "He sat at table five that night," she said. "It is in the corner and overlooks the dining room and the bar. He could sit there and see everyone in the restaurant." As always, she said, Hemingway ordered a bottle of Bordeaux wine with his meal and Mary ordered a martini. "He didn't act any differently that night. He sat very quietly. I never knew him to be anything but a very gentle man."

Early the next morning, Ernest arose at daybreak and quietly went down the carpeted stairway to the basement and selected a double-barreled shotgun from his collection. He loaded both barrels and returned to the front foyer of the house, just off the living room. In the light of the bright, Idaho daybreak, he ended his life.

Last Supper

New York strip steak

baked potato

Caesar salad

Bordeaux wine

JIMI HENDRIX

Guitarist

1942—1970

EARLY IN JIMI HENDRIX's career, critics called him the "black Elvis." That dubious title faded with time as Hendrix created his own persona and earned his own niche in rock 'n' roll history as a guitarist without peer. His hyperamplified style was not appreciated by everyone, but by the time of his death he was revered by the underground 1960s youth culture. Only after his death did he receive widespread recognition as one of the founding fathers of a style that became known as heavy metal. Typically, he used two amplifiers when he performed and turned the volume up to the maximum. One night, it was reported, he "burned up" four amplifiers. He attracted attention at the 1967 Monterey Pop Festival by burning his guitar onstage. In the final three years of his life, he recorded four gold albums: *Are You Experienced?*, *Electric Ladyland, Axis: Bold as Love,* and *Smash Hits.* On September 18, 1970, Hendrix ate a tuna fish sandwich prepared by his companion, Monika Dannemann. They talked until 6 A.M., and then went to bed. Hendrix never awoke.

Last Supper

Tuna fish sandwich

BILLIE HOLIDAY

Recording Artist

1915–1959

Forty years after her death, Billie Holiday is revered as one of the greatest female jazz singers of all time. She began her career in 1933 by recording two songs with the Benny Goodman orchestra. Two years later, while fronting for Count Basie, she was told her skin was too light to allow her to perform with black bands. She heeded that advice and successfully auditioned for Artie Shaw's band, becoming the first black vocalist to work with a white orchestra. The next decade was creatively and financially productive for her; she was the highest-paid nightclub performer in New York. But it was emotionally draining; she was not allowed to use the main entrance in hotels and nightclubs in which she performed. Most entertainers of that and subsequent eras have called her one of the most influential entertainers in American history. Frank Sinatra, who was a frequent member of her audience, once said she was the single greatest influence on his career. Unfortunately, Billie Holiday's last days did not reflect the victories of her earlier years. On May 30, 1959, she collapsed while her friend, Frankie Freedom, was serving her a bowl of custard and oatmeal. She later went into a coma and was taken to a hospital. She emerged from the coma long enough for "friends" to feed her illegal drugs. On July 10 she was allowed to receive gifts of candy and ice cream and fruit. After enjoying the treats, she relapsed and lingered until July 17. At the time of her death, her net estate was valued at $1,345.36.

Last Supper

Candy

Ice cream

Fresh fruit

HOWARD HUGHES

Aviator / Movie Mogul / Entrepreneur

1905–1976

THE STORY OF HOWARD HUGHES's demise is well known: one of the world's wealthiest men living out his final days in isolation and squalor, seemingly without a friend in the world. In his final years he lived the life of a hermit and went for a 20-year period without ever being photographed or seen in public. He allowed no visitors, trusted no one, and communicated with only a handful of aides. He refused to talk to anyone by telephone, depending instead upon written memos and notes. In better years he was the toast of Hollywood, where he dated beautiful actresses, enjoyed a lavish lifestyle, and reveled in his reputation as an accomplished pilot. By the 1960s he was a major player in Las Vegas, where he acquired several high-profile hotels and casinos. In his final days his weight was down to 93 pounds, and his primary diet consisted of 150 milligrams of liquid Valium and codeine. His last documented dinner was on March 30, 1976: It consisted of a glass of milk, which took eight hours to drink. An autopsy determined no actual cause of death. All his vital organs were still functioning at adequate levels. Doctors concluded that he probably starved to death.

Last Supper

Glass of milk

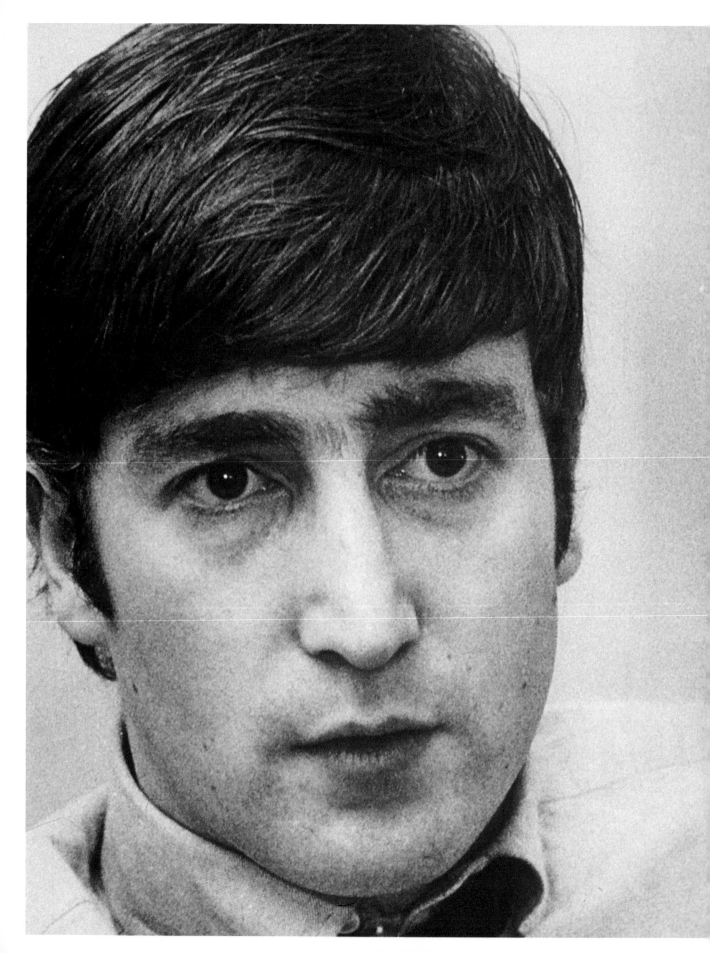

JOHN LENNON

Recording Artist

1940–1980

RINGO WAS THE FUNNY BEATLE. George the quiet one. Paul the pretty one. John was … well, the one who was all of the above and none of the above. When the Beatles broke up, he was the first to release a solo single, "Give Peace a Chance," in July 1969. But the artistic freedom he expected to find upon his separation from the group was slow to arrive. He placed several singles on the charts over the next few years, including "Imagine," but not until late 1974, with the release of "Whatever Gets You Thru the Night," was he able to claim his first number one as a solo artist. In his private life things were not going well at all. He separated from Yoko and found himself in a battle with American immigration authorities over his application to remain in the country. In 1975 it was the birth of his son, Sean, that seemed to bring everything to a head. John took one look at his infant son, walked away from his recording career, and devoted the next five years of his life to being a househusband. In 1980 he and Yoko composed about two dozen songs while they were on vacation in Bermuda. When they returned, they booked time at the Hit Factory studio, recorded the songs, and then pitched them to several record labels. Geffen accepted the album, *Double Fantasy*, sight unseen. The first single from the album, "(Just Like) Starting Over," promptly zoomed up the charts, giving John his second solo number one hit. On December 8, 1980, John had a late lunch at the Stage Deli in New York. Manager Gill Kashkin recalls his ordering a corned beef sandwich and hot tea. It is the last documented meal John had. Later that day he and Yoko went to the studio to mix a song titled "Walking on Thin Ice." It was upon his return to his Manhattan apartment building that evening that he was gunned down by an assassin.

Last Supper

Corned beef sandwich

Hot tea

HUEY "KINGFISH" LONG

United States Senator/Governor of Louisiana

1893–1935

WHILE VISITING THE LOUISIANA STATE CAPITOL on September 8, 1935, Huey Long, or "Kingfish," as he was known to friends and enemies alike, was felled by a single bullet from a lone assassin. Carl Weiss, a 29-year-old physician, was shot to death at the scene in a hail of gunfire from Long's bodyguards. Weiss was identified by the police as the killer, but over the years doubts have surfaced about his guilt. In 1991 Weiss's remains were exhumed and examined by a team of forensic scientists, whose report expressed grave doubts about the government's case against the physician. At the time of his death, Long was considered the Ross Perot of American politics, a populist who was a potent threat to President Franklin D. Roosevelt's reelection. In September 1935 he seemed on the verge of building a national base as an independent candidate for the presidency. On the day before his assassination, he drove to Baton Rouge and spent the night at his capital apartment. The following evening, before being escorted to the Capitol by an army of bodyguards, he enjoyed a light dinner in the privacy of his apartment.

Last Supper

Cheese and crackers

Fresh fruit

MARILYN MONROE

Actress/Cultural Icon

1926–1962

Marilyn Monroe was more than just an actress. With a haunting mixture of sex appeal and emotional vulnerability, she was both the embodiment of the American Dream and an enduring symbol of all things unattainable in American society. The fact that she married two of the era's dominant, but in some ways opposing, male influences—baseball great Joe DiMaggio and playwright Arthur Miller—gave her life even more of a storybook appearance. Her final hours are still the subject of controversy and debate. Did she die of a drug overdose? If so, was it suicide? If not, was it accidental? Was it murder? With the passing of time, the mystery of her death only seems to grow. The official cause of death was attributed to a drug overdose, but there are reasons to doubt that, especially in view of the autopsy report, which seems to contradict that finding. Her last documented meal was at a Brentwood restaurant, where she ate a Mexican buffet and awaited a luncheon guest who never arrived.

Last Supper

Guacamole

Stuffed mushrooms

Spicy meatballs

Dom Perignon Champagne

ELVIS PRESLEY

Entertainer

1935–1977

I N 1977 ELVIS PRESLEY was approaching the quarter-century mark of his career. He had resumed his concert appearances, but his recording successes had become infrequent, and hit records seemed a thing of the past. Elvis's life was in a shambles. His manager, Colonel Tom Parker, was drawing a 50 percent commission, making it increasingly difficult for Elvis to maintain the lifestyle to which he had become accustomed. His abuse of prescription drugs was escalating. He and his father had become caught up in an organized crime sting that would require them to testify in federal criminal proceedings. It is not surprising that his personal life was also in a mess. His divorce from Priscilla had been painful and had exacted an emotional toll. In August his daughter, Lisa Marie, was visiting him at Graceland. On the afternoon of August 15, he played games with Lisa Marie and entertained himself at his piano. As was his custom, he stayed up all night. At 4 A.M. the cook served him what would be his last meal. After eating a dish of ice cream with cookies served by Pauline Nicholson, the cook, he played racquetball for a couple of hours. Before turning in, Elvis went into the bathroom. His girlfriend, Ginger Alden, admonished him not to fall asleep, as he was apt to do. It was the last conversation he ever had. At around 2:25 that afternoon, Elvis was found dead on the bathroom floor.

Last Supper

Ice Cream

Cookies

FRANKLIN D. ROOSEVELT

Thirty-second President of the United States

1882–1945

F RANKLIN DELANO ROOSEVELT was to Americans of the 20th century what Abraham Lincoln was to the 19th century and George Washington was to the 18th century: A larger-than-life figure upon whose shoulders was balanced the collective hopes of the entire nation. Even so, Roosevelt spent much of his political career deceiving the public about his physical condition—he was a paraplegic—and his extramarital relationship with Mrs. Lucy Rutherfurd. The news media acquiesced in the president's deceptions.

Because of his paralysis, Roosevelt sought various treatments over the years to ease his discomfort and increase his mobility. In early April 1945 Roosevelt left his wife, Eleanor, in Washington and traveled to a spa in Warm Springs, Georgia, with Mrs. Rutherfurd and his usual entourage. On April 12, as the president sat looking over papers spread out on a bridge table, he was brought his lunch—warm oatmeal prepared in milk. He hated the taste of it, but his physician thought it would be good for him. After only a couple of spoonfuls, he pushed it aside and returned to his paperwork.

Sitting across from him was Mrs. Rutherfurd. At one point, with his hand shaking, he rubbed his fingers across his forehead. "I have a terrible headache," he complained. As she watched in horror, he slumped in his chair, his regal figure draped in his trademark cape. Roosevelt was lifted from his chair and taken to his bedroom. His physician rushed to his side and discovered that the president had suffered a stroke. As Roosevelt lay dying, Mrs. Rutherfurd was ordered to leave the house so as not to bring scandal upon the presidency. Roosevelt died without ever regaining consciousness, the taste of the dreaded oatmeal still upon his lips.

Last Supper

Warm oatmeal with milk

Engraved by T. W. Hunt.

From a Dag. by Brady.

ZACHARY TAYLOR

Twelfth President of the United States

1784–1850

IT WAS THE FOURTH OF JULY 1850. As part of the festivities, President Zachary Taylor walked from the White House over to the site of the future Washington Monument, where he dedicated the cornerstone for what promised to be an impressive tribute to America's first president. It was a blistering, steamy day, and after spending two hours outside in the heat, Taylor decided to walk back to the White House by way of the Potomac River. Perhaps he thought a cooling breeze would be coming in off the river. Perhaps, since he was alone, he simply wanted time to ponder the issues of the day quietly. Whatever the reason, he took the long way home.

Historically, it was a time of crisis for Taylor. At issue was the admission of California as a "free" state, one in which slavery would be prohibited. The slave states were opposed, since it would upset the balance of power and give the free states a majority of votes in Congress. If California were to be admitted as a free state, supporters of slavery wanted New Mexico admitted as a slave state. Taylor was opposed to slavery and was not in favor of pairing California with New Mexico. He was in for the fight of his political life.

When he arrived at the White House, he enjoyed a bowl of cherries and drank a glass of cold milk. A short time later he became violently ill. He lingered for five days, unable to keep anything in his stomach. Upon his death rumors persisted that he was murdered by someone who put arsenic in his bowl of cherries. Today, some historians still believe that. Others say he simply got a bad bowl of cherries.

Last Supper

Bowl of cherries

Glass of cold milk

JAMES THURBER

Humorist / Illustrator / Author

1894–1961

I N 1955, SIX YEARS BEFORE his own death, James Thurber, who was famous for his dog caricatures in the *New Yorker*, wrote about the death of his poodle: "I know now, and knew then, that no dog is fond of dying, but I have never had a dog that showed a human, jittery fear of death, either. Death, to a dog, is the final unavoidable compulsion, the last ineluctable scent on a fearsome trail, but they like to face it alone, going out into the woods, among the leaves, if there are any leaves when their time comes, enduring without sentimental human distraction the Last Loneliness, which they are wise enough to know cannot be shared by anyone."

When the time came for his own death, Thurber once joked, he suspected his wife, Helen, would be at the hairdresser. As fate would have it, the humorist's death would fall far short of the passing he envisioned for his canine friends. His final days were spent at Doctors Hospital in New York, where he underwent brain surgery and later developed pneumonia and a blood clot in his lung. Surrounded by doctors and nurses, who prodded, poked, and invaded his personal space, he lapsed into a deep coma. As the end drew near, his head was raised from his pillow, and he was given a sip of brandy, a pleasure that on other occasions had always worked miracles.

But there were no miracles for Thurber on that day. He died gasping for breath, neither alone nor in the midst of an autumnal bed of leaves, but surrounded by the cold, medical realities of modern technology. As he had predicted, his wife, Helen, was sitting under a dryer at the hairdresser when she got the news.

Last Supper

A sip of brandy

ACKNOWLEDGMENTS

I would like to thank the following people for their help with this book: Jim Barkley, who set the project in motion; my publisher, Geoff Golson, who may be the first publishing executive ever to negotiate a book proposal from beginning to end entirely by e-mail; my editors, Paul Frumkin and Frank Scatoni; and Barbara Pisani, Amy Striebel, Patrick Robinson, Scott Tolley, Sally Irwin, Francesca Brooks, Bert Holman, Joy Pinto, Emily Jacobs, Milton B. Suchin, Karen Ring Borgstrom, Ben Payne, Suzie Rosenberg, the staff at William Alexander Percy Library, Rebecca Freedman at the Aktkins Center, the Jean and Alexander Heard Library at Vanderbilt University, Jeff Abraham, Chris Bender, Jane Mallea, Camilla Rothwell, Thurman Boykin, Darenda Owens, Gina Gargano, Amy Rosenthal, Gill Kashkin, Larry Schwartz, Lucy Sholley, Audrey Butler, Sue Moskowitz, my mother, and, of course, all the celebrities who contributed to the book.

PHOTO CREDITS

Karen McDougal/photo courtesy of *Playboy*

Trent Lott/photo courtesy of Trent Lott

Elvis Presley dressed as arab/MGM publicity

Joe Eszterhas/photo by Naomi Eszterhas

Crystal Bernard/Archive Newsphotos

Bill Clinton/photo courtesy *Nation's Restaurant News*

James Dean/Archive Photos

Marcia Ball/courtesy Rounder Records

Jack Nicklaus/photo courtesy *Nation's Restaurant News*

Terri Clark/photo by Matthew Barnes/courtesy Mercury Records

Betty White/photo by Ralph Merlino/Archive Photos

Princess Diana/Archive Photos

Rosemary Clooney/Archive Photos

Helen Reddy/photo by Tim Boxer/Archive Photos

John Elway/photo by Ron Sachs/Archive Photos

Marilyn Monroe/Archive Photos

Fred de Cordova/Jerry Lowe/SAGA/Archive Photos

John Andretti/courtesy John Andretti/Photo © Dorsey Patrick

Brenda Lee (portrait)/courtesy Brenda Lee

Todd English/photo courtesy Todd English

Dan Evins/photo courtesy Dan Evins

Abe Gustin/photo courtesy Abe Gustin

Tom T. Hall/photo by James Dickerson

Steve Spurrier/photo by Pierre DuCharme/Archive Photos

John Lennon/Popperfoto/Archive Photos

Nora Pouillon (portrait)/photo by Daniel Hahdavian/courtesy Nora Pouillon

Daniel Boulud (portrait)/courtesy Daniel Boulud

Daniel Boulud postcard of Café Boulud/courtesy Daniel Boulud

Zachary Taylor/Archive Photos

Roland Passot/courtesy Roland Passot

Phyllis Diller/courtesy Phyllis Diller

Arnold Palmer/Archive Photos

George Zimmer/photo courtesy George Zimmer

Rosie O'Donnell/Archive Photos

Jimi Hendrix/Archive Photos

Dr. John/photo byAndy Earl/courtesy Virgin Records

Crystal Gayle/Frank Driggs Collection/Archive Photos

John Candy/SAGA/S. Johnson/Archive Photos

Billy Burnette/publicity photo

Hale Irwin/photo courtesy Hale Irwin © PGA Tour

Greg Norman/photo courtesy Greg Norman

Norman Van Aken/photo courtesy of Norman Van Aken

Amazing Kreskin/photo courtesy Amazing Kreskin

Vanna White/photo by Timothy White/courtesy *Wheel of Fortune*

Huey Long/Archive Photos

Paul Anka/photo by Patrick DeMervelec/courtesy Epic Records

Gregg Allman/photo by Jeff Dunas

Tom Douglas/photo courtesy Tom Douglas

Howard Hughes/Archive Photos

Ann Coulter/photo courtesy Regnery Publishing

Dick Clark/Archive Photos

Scotty Moore/photo by James Dickerson

Patti Page/Frank Driggs Collection/Archive Photos

Billie Holiday/Frank Driggs Collection/Archive Photos

Rhonda Shear/courtesy Rhonda Shear

Reggie White/Reuters/Gary Hershorn/Archive Photos

Bobby Bowden/photo by Jeff Christensen/Archive Photos

Ernest Hemingway/Popperfoto/Archive Photos

Eileen Fulton/obtained by publisher

Faye Kellerman/photo by Jonathan Exley/courtesy Faye Kellerman

Carl Reiner/Archive Photos

James Dickerson/photo courtesy James Dickerson

Dr. Robert Atkins/photo courtesy Dr. Robert Atkins

Stephan Pyles/photo courtesy Stephan Pyles

James Thurber/Archive Photos

Franklin D. Roosevelt/Archive Photos

Mario Ferrari/courtesy Mario Ferrari

Cammi Granato/Reuters/Gary Hershorn/Archive Photos

Mike Ditka/Reuters/Sue Ogrocki/Archive Photos

John McCain/Reuters/Gary Cameron/Archive Photos

Fred Thompson/Archive Photos

RECIPE INDEX